PRELUDE TO WAR

A SOURCEBOOK ON THE CIVIL WAR

PRELUDE TO WAR

A SOURCEBOOK ON THE CIVIL WAR

Edited by Carter Smith

AMERICAN ALBUMS FROM THE COLLECTIONS OF
THE LIBRARY OF CONGRESS

THE MILLBROOK PRESS, *Brookfield, Connecticut*

Cover: "Henry Clay Addressing the Senate, 1850." Drawing by Peter Rothermel, 1855.

Title Page: "A Cotton Plantation on the Mississippi." Lithograph by Currier & Ives, 1884.

Contents Page: Know-Nothing soap label. Lithograph by Geo. A. Hill and Co., 1854.

Back Cover: Jarrett & Palmer London Company Playbill of "Uncle Tom's Cabin." Lithograph by W. J. Morgan and Co., nineteenth century.

Library of Congress Cataloging-in-Publication Data

Prelude to war : a sourcebook on the Civil War / edited by Carter Smith.
     p. cm. — (American albums from the collections of the Library of
Congress)
     Includes bibliographical references and index.
     Summary: Uses a variety of contemporary materials to describe and
illustrate the causes of the Civil War that developed between 1820 and 1861.
     ISBN 1-56294-261-1 (lib. bdg.)
     1. United States—History—Civil War, 1861–1865—Causes—Juvenile
literature. 2. United States—History—Civil War, 1861–1865—Causes—
Pictorial works—Juvenile literature. 3. United States—History—Civil War,
1861–1865—Causes—Sources—Juvenile literature. [1. United States—
History—Civil War, 1861–1865—Causes—Sources.] I. Smith, C. Carter. II.
Series.
E459.P74 1993
973.7'11'0222—dc20   92-16545
                                                                CIP
                                                                 AC

 Created in association with Media Projects Incorporated

C. Carter Smith, *Executive Editor*
Lelia Wardwell, *Managing Editor*
Charles A. Wills, *Principal Writer*
Kimberly Horstman, *Picture and Production Editor*
Lydia Link, *Designer*
Athena Angelos, *Photo Researcher*

The consultation of Bernard F. Reilly, Jr., Head Curator of the Prints and
Photographs Division of the Library of Congress, is gratefully acknowledged.

Contents

In the North, agriculture usually meant small, family-run farms, such as the one shown in this Currier & Ives print titled "The Farmer's Home—Harvest." At harvest time, Northern farmers used paid laborers—not slaves—to help them with the extra work.

Introduction

PRELUDE TO WAR is one of the volumes in a series published by The Millbrook Press titled AMERICAN ALBUMS FROM THE COLLECTIONS OF THE LIBRARY OF CONGRESS and one of six books in the series subtitled SOURCEBOOKS ON THE CIVIL WAR.

The editors' basic goal for the series is to make available to the student many of the original visual documents preserved in the Library of Congress as records of the American past. The volumes in THE CIVIL WAR series reproduce many of the prints, broadsides, maps, and other works preserved in the Library's special collections divisions, and a few from its general book collections. Most prominently featured in this series are the holdings of the Prints and Photographs Division.

PRELUDE TO WAR covers an important era in the history of American graphic art. It was an era of increasing appreciation for the persuasive power of pictures. Many of the images of Northern industry shown here were produced for merchants and manufacturers for publicity or advertising purposes. (Industrial images of the South from this period are not so plentiful, since the Southern economy was predominantly agricultural.) The propaganda value of pictures was also important to the Mexican War effort. Prints of battles and leaders pro-

duced during that conflict were part of an effort to glorify war, which, although popular among the merchants of the North and planters of the South, was essentially an unprovoked act of military aggression.

Images were an especially important weapon in the campaign against slavery. The abolitionists used broadsides, illustrated pamphlets, almanacs, and prints in an attempt to convince Northerners of the evils of the slave system. In response, their opponents published prints ridiculing African Americans and the antislavery contingent. When events in Kansas brought the issue of slavery to a head, political cartoons conveyed the bitterness of anti-Southern feeling.

Photography came of age during the Civil War as a recorder of national life. Although the medium was introduced as early as 1839, it was only with the Civil War that it became widely used as a means of reporting events. Mathew Brady's photograph of Abraham Lincoln's inauguration in 1861 opened a new era in the documentation of American history.

The works reproduced here represent a small but telling portion of the rich pictorial record of the Civil War preserved by the Library of Congress in its role as the nation's library.

BERNARD F. REILLY, JR.

By the time of the Civil War, the United States comprised three distinct regions—the North, the South, and the West.

The traditional boundary line separating North and South was the Mason-Dixon line of 1769, establishing the border between Maryland and Pennsylvania. In 1784, the line was extended westward to include Virginia.

The Ohio River became another dividing line in 1787, with the passage of the Northwest Ordinance. This document organized the land between the Great Lakes and the Ohio River into the Northwest Territory. It also prohibited slavery in the area. The land south of the Northwest Territory, however, joined the Union as the states of Kentucky and Tennessee, with state constitutions permitting slavery.

Between 1783 and 1853, the nation's western boundary leaped from the Mississippi River to the Pacific Ocean. The Louisiana Purchase of 1803 added about 530,000 square miles of land and extended the frontier to the Rocky Mountains.

The next large territory added to the United States was Texas. Once part of Mexico, then an independent republic, Texas became a state in December 1845. Following the American victory in the Mexican War of 1846–48, Mexico yielded its western provinces, which extended to the Pacific Ocean, to the United States.

In 1846, the Oregon Territory was added to the Union. Eight years later, Congress purchased a strip of Mexican land along the southern border of present-day Arizona and New Mexico. This land, called the "Gadsden Purchase," filled out the now-familiar outline of the continental United States.

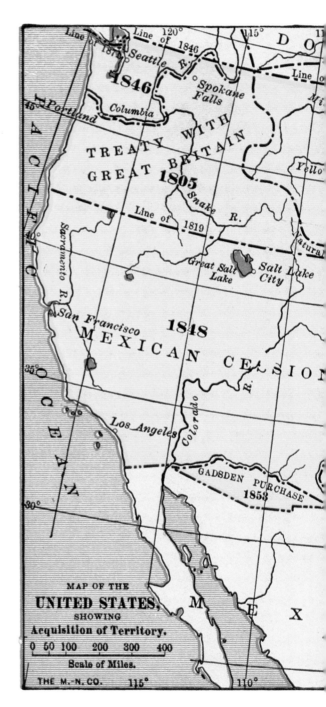

MAP OF THE
UNITED STATES,
SHOWING
Acquisition of Territory.
0   50 100   200   300   400
Scale of Miles.
THE M.-N. CO.

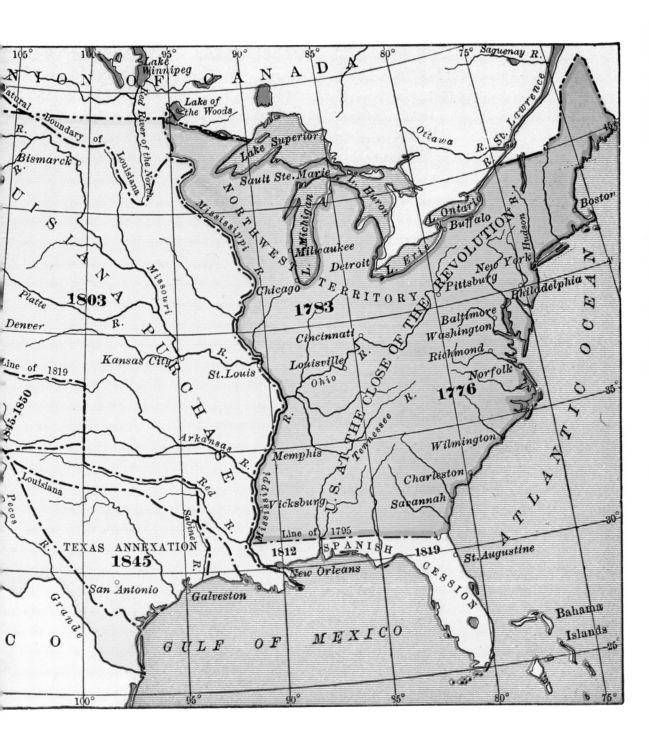

NION OF CANADA

105° 100° 95° Lake Winnipeg 90° 85° 80° 75° Saguenay R.

Natural Boundary of Louisiana

Bismarck

R. R.

LOUISIANA

Red River of the North

Lake of the Woods

Lake Superior

Sault Ste. Marie

Mississippi R.

NORTHWEST

L. Michigan

L. Huron

Milwaukee

Detroit

Chicago

Ottawa R.

R. St. Lawrence

45°

L. Ontario

Buffalo

L. Erie

Hudson R.

Boston

New York

Pittsburg

Philadelphia

1803

Platte R.

Denver

PURCHASE

Missouri R.

TERRITORY

1783

Cincinnati

Louisville

Ohio R.

Baltimore

Washington

Richmond

Line of 1819

Kansas City

St. Louis

R.

Arkansas R.

Norfolk

1776

35°

REVOLUTION

U.S. AT THE CLOSE OF THE

Tennessee R.

Wilmington

1855–1850

Memphis

Mississippi R.

Vicksburg

Red R.

Sabine R.

Charleston

Savannah

30°

Louisiana

Pecos R.

TEXAS ANNEXATION

1845

San Antonio

Galveston

Line of 1795

1812

SPANISH

New Orleans

CESSION

1819

St. Augustine

ATLANTIC OCEAN

Rio Grande

C O

GULF   OF   MEXICO

Bahama Islands

25°

100° 95° 90° 85° 80° 75°

A TIMELINE OF MAJOR EVENTS
1820–1830

WORLD HISTORY

1820 Liberia is established in West Africa. The nation's American founders hope it will provide a homeland for freed slaves and other American blacks.

1820–21 Five Central and South American nations—Venezuela, Peru, Guatemala, Panama, and Santo Domingo—gain independence from Spain.

1821 General Augustin de Iturbide leads his forces through Mexico, challenging Spanish viceroys and declaring Mexico independent.

Freed slaves departing for Liberia

AMERICAN HISTORY AND CULTURE

1820 The national census shows the population of the U.S. to be almost 10 million.

1821 The Troy Female Seminary, the first women's college in the United States, opens its doors in Troy, New York.

1823 On December 2, President James Monroe proclaims what becomes known as the Monroe Doctrine; it states that the U.S. will oppose European attempts to interfere with the domestic affairs of North and South America.

President James Monroe

1824 No candidate receives a majority of the popular vote in the presidential election; the House of Representatives breaks the deadlock by declaring John Quincy Adams of Massachusetts the winner.

1825 The Erie Canal opens in November as the first boat from Buffalo arrives in New York Harbor. The canal links the

SLAVERY AND SECESSION

1820 Eighty-six free blacks sail from New York to Sierra Leone on the West African coast. The venture is sponsored by the American Colonization Society, which hopes to return American blacks to Africa.

•Congress states that the slave trade is considered piracy and that slave traders will face the death penalty if captured. (Importing slaves became illegal in 1808 under a clause added to the Constitution.)

•The laws known as the Compromise of 1820 pass Congress. Maine is admitted as a free state, Missouri as a slave state, and slavery is forbidden in the West, north of Missouri's southern border (latitude 36' 30").

1824 Congress passes the first of several Tariff Acts in May. These economic measures tend to favor the industrial North over the agricultural South, causing bitter resentment among Southerners in Congress.

1825 A small group of liberals in Russia attempts to overthrow the Czarist government; the movement fails and its leaders are executed.
•The *shogun* (supreme ruler) of Japan forbids all foreign ships from entering into Japanese waters, thus strengthening

Japan's isolation from the rest of the world.

1826 Simón Bolívar, leader of many of the independence movements in Central and South America, calls a conference of newly independent states in Panama. The conference fails to unite the new states.

1828 Shaka, the brilliant warrior who led the southern African Zulu nation on several successful conquests, is assassinated by his brothers.

1829 The Treaty of Adrianapole settles the conflict between the European nations and the Ottoman Empire;

Turkish influence on the European mainland declines, and Greece wins its independence.

1830 Revolution in France ends the conservative rule of King Charles X. Louis Philippe, the Duke of Orleans, replaces him in a constitutional monarchy.

Great Lakes with the Atlantic Ocean and makes the shipment of western goods to eastern markets cheaper and easier.

1826 The first commercial railroad in the U.S., the Baltimore & Ohio, opens for business.
•Andrew Jackson, a hero of the War

The Erie Canal

of 1812 from Tennessee, defeats John Quincy Adams in the presidential election.

1830 The Church of Latter-Day Saints, later known as the Mormons, is organized in western

New York State by Joseph Smith.
•The Indian Removal Act becomes law. The measure calls for the Cherokee, Chickasaw, Choctaw, Creek, and Seminole tribes of the Southeastern states to be relocated to an "Indian Territory" west of the Mississippi River.

Title page of Walker's Appeal

1827 New York State abolishes slavery; over 10,000 blacks are freed.

1828 Responding to a new Tariff Act, South Carolina's legislature declares that states have the right to "nullify" federal laws which they believe to be unconstitutional.

1829 An anonymous pamphlet, *Walker's Appeal*, is published. The document (which urges slaves to revolt against their masters) causes anger in the South.

1830 After a long debate with South Carolina senator Robert Hayne,

Daniel Webster of Massachusetts declares, "Liberty and Union, now and forever!" The statement becomes a rallying cry for supporters of a strong Union.

A TIMELINE OF MAJOR EVENTS
1831–1840

WORLD HISTORY

1833 After decades of effort by slavery's opponents, an act of Parliament bans slavery in any part of the British Empire. The act goes into effect in 1834.
•General López de Santa Anna rises to power in Mexico. He is the latest in a series of dictators since the country won its independence from Spain.
•British mathematician Charles Babbage outlines the workings of an "analytical engine." The engine is never constructed, but his principles lay the foundation for the modern digital computer.

1837 French-speaking Canadians in Lower Canada (what is now Quebec) rebel against British rule in an unsuccessful uprising led by Louis-Joseph Papineau.

1838 Nineteen-year-old Victoria is crowned Queen of England; during her sixty-three-year

AMERICAN HISTORY AND CULTURE

Black Hawk

1831 Sauk and Fox Indians in Illinois, led by Chief Black Hawk, attempt an uprising against white settlers; it fails after the outnumbered Indian forces are defeated and scattered along the Bad Axe River in Wisconsin.
•Cyrus McCormick invents the reaper, a harvesting machine, and revolutionizes farming throughout the world.

1832 Nominated by the newly formed Democratic Party, Andrew Jackson is reelected president of the United States.

1833 The *New York Sun*, the first successful daily newspaper, is founded; an issue costs one penny.

1834 Abraham Lincoln enters politics for the first time, joining the assembly of the Illinois legislature at the age of twenty-five.

SLAVERY AND SECESSION

1831 Virginia slave Nat Turner leads an uprising that leaves fifty-seven whites dead. Many blacks, including Turner, are executed in response, and Southern states pass harsh laws restricting slave conduct.
•South Carolina passes an Ordinance of Nullification opposing federal tariffs. Some leaders propose to secede. President Jackson announces he will use force to keep South Carolina in the Union.

The discovery of Nat Turner

•William Lloyd Garrison begins publishing *The Liberator*, soon to be America's chief abolitionist journal.

reign, Britain becomes the world's greatest colonial power.

1839 The first Opium War begins between Britain and China; after Britain's victory in 1842, China is forced to give up Hong Kong and to award special privileges to British merchants.

The Opium War

1840 British financier Samuel Cunard begins the first scheduled steamship service between Europe and North America.
•Britain signs the Treaty of Waitangi with the Maoris, the native inhabitants of New Zealand. The treaty officially establishes the islands as a British colony.

1835 Ohio's Oberlin College, already unusual because it admits women students, announces it will offer education to blacks as well.
•The Seminole War begins in Florida when Seminole Indians refuse to leave their homeland and to surrender escaped slaves living among them.

•The national debt is paid off as a result of revenues from increased railroad construction and skyrocketing land values.

1836 Democrat Martin Van Buren defeats several other candidates and succeeds Andrew Jackson as president.

•Despite initial setbacks at the Alamo and Goliad, American settlers in Texas succeed in breaking away from Mexico. Former Tennessee governor Sam Houston becomes Texas's first president.

1837 Mount Holyoke, the first permanent college for women, is founded in Massachusetts.

1840 The population of the United States reaches 17 million.

1833 The American Anti-Slavery Society is founded in New York City. It becomes the largest and best known abolitionist organization, printing and circulating many publications opposing slavery.

1834 Authorities in Charleston, South Carolina, uncover plans for a slave uprising. Thirty-four blacks are executed, including the conspiracy's leader, freed slave Denmark Vesey.

1836 Under pressure from Southern politicians, Congress passes a "gag rule," which essentially forbids Congress from considering or even discussing anti-slavery petitions.

1837 Elijah Lovejoy, editor of the *St. Louis Observer,* an abolitionist newspaper, is killed by a proslavery mob in Alton, Illinois.

1838 Robert Purvis assumes leadership of the Underground Railroad, the network of abolitionists and free blacks who help escaped slaves reach the free states and Canada.

A TIMELINE OF MAJOR EVENTS
1841–1850

WORLD HISTORY

1843 Slavery continues to thrive in parts of Latin America; Cuba's slave population is estimated to be over 400,000.

1844 British authorities find Daniel O'Connell guilty of plotting to overthrow British rule in Ireland.

•The eastern part of the Caribbean island nation of Haiti secedes and becomes the Dominican Republic.

1845 A famine breaks out in Ireland when disease strikes the potato crop, the country's staple food. Over the next decade, a

Slaves in Latin America

million starve; hundreds of thousands emigrate to other nations.

1846 British and French astronomers simultaneously discover a new planet;

AMERICAN HISTORY AND CULTURE

1841 After little more than a month in office, President Harrison dies and is succeeded by Vice President John Tyler.

1842 The Seminole War ends as the last free Seminole bands are forced to move to Indian

President John Tyler

Territory (what is now Oklahoma).

•U.S. and British representatives sign the Webster-Ashburton Treaty. The document settles long-standing disputes over the exact border between British territory (Canada) and the U.S.

•A wagon train of forty-seven people leaves Missouri for California in May,

finally arriving in November. Their journey marks the beginning of a great movement west.

•Artist and inventor Samuel F. B. Morse develops a working electric telegraph.

•The first large groups of settlers reach the Oregon country along the route later known

SLAVERY AND SECESSION

1843 American and British diplomats agree to conduct joint naval patrols along the African coast in an effort to stop the slave trade.

1844 After years of effort by former president John

Quincy Adams, now a representative from Massachusetts, the Congressional "gag rule" is overturned.

•The Baptist Church divides into Northern and Southern groups over the issue of slavery; splits later

occur in the Methodist and Presbyterian churches.

1845 Escaped slave and abolitionist Frederick Douglass publishes his autobiography. Controversy over the book leads Douglass to leave the United States temporarily for Britain.

1846 Representative David Wilmot of Pennsylvania asks that a clause forbidding slavery in any lands won from Mexico be attached to a Congressional spending bill. The spending bill eventually passes—without the anti-slavery clause.

at first called "Planet X," it is later named Neptune.
•A Polish revolt against Russian and Austrian occupying troops ends when both nations capture the city of Kraków.

1847 British troops defeat the Xhosa nation of South Africa, further

securing British control of the region.

1848 Dissatisfied with repressive governments and poor economic conditions, students and intellectuals lead revolutions in Germany, Italy, and other European nations. These liberal movements fail to win most of their goals.

•In the aftermath of the Revolutions of 1848, Karl Marx and Friedrich Engels publish *The Communist Manifesto*. The pamphlet outlines the economic and political philosophy which becomes the basis for modern Communism.
•The Taiping Rebellion erupts in China; it is an

uprising against the nation's corrupt Ch'ing rulers.

1850 Britain's Parliament grants a large measure of self-government to Australia. The colony had originally been founded as an island prison for criminals from the British Isles.

---

as the Oregon Trail. Oregon at this time is jointly governed by the U.S. and Great Britain.

1844 Democrat James Polk defeats Whig candidate Henry Clay in the presidential election.

1845 The Republic of Texas is annexed

to the U.S., increasing tensions with Mexico.

1846 After receiving news of a skirmish between U.S. and Mexican forces in May, President Polk asks Congress for a declaration of war. Taylor's forces win a string of victories throughout the summer.

•The "Bear Flag Revolt" begins in the Mexican province of California, as American settlers declare the region an independent republic. California is quickly annexed to the U.S.

1848 The Treaty of Guadalupe Hidalgo officially ends the

Mexican War. Mexico surrenders territories to the U.S., including part of California, Arizona, New Mexico, Nevada, Utah, and Colorado.

1850 President Taylor dies; Vice President Millard Fillmore takes office.

1848 Antislavery Democrats form the Free Soil Party in Buffalo, New York.

1849 Maryland slave Harriet Tubman escapes to the North. She returns to the South many times to help other slaves escape.

Map of the Compromise of 1850

1850 The Compromise of 1850 is passed by Congress in March. California is admitted as a free state; Utah and New Mexico are made territories with their slavery status undecided; and a new, stronger Fugitive Slave Act goes into effect.

A TIMELINE OF MAJOR EVENTS
1851–1861

WORLD HISTORY

1853 Fear of Russian influence in Eastern Europe leads Britain and France to side with the Ottoman Empire against Russia. These tensions lead to the Crimean War, fought mostly in the Crimean Peninsula on the Black Sea in Russia.

1854 China's Taiping Rebellion ends with the fall of Nanking to a European-trained Manchu army. The rebellion has cost the lives of 20 million Chinese.

1856 Henry Bessemer of Great Britain devises a new and more efficient process for making steel.
•The Treaty of Paris ends the Crimean War in a victory for the Allies (Britain, France, and the Ottoman Empire).

1857 The Sepoy Rebellion, a revolt against British rule, begins in India. The uprising is put down a year later.

1859 British scientist Charles Darwin publishes *On the Origin of Species*, which outlines radical new theories of evolution and natural selection.
•British philosopher John Stuart Mill publishes his influential essay *On Liberty*. Mill argues that the duty of government is to work for the

AMERICAN HISTORY AND CULTURE

1851 A naval squadron commanded by Commodore Matthew C. Perry arrives in Japan. Sent to open the long-closed nation to American trade, Perry succeeds when the Japanese government signs a treaty the following year.

•Mexico sells a strip of land (now part of New Mexico and Arizona) to the U.S. for $10 million; the purchase is negotiated by James B. Gadsden of South Carolina, who hopes the land will become the route of a transcontinental railroad

Mathew Brady

from the South to the West Coast.

1852 Democrat Franklin Pierce wins the presidential election, defeating Whig candidate Winfield Scott.

1853 Mathew Brady, later a major photographer of the Civil War, opens his first

SLAVERY AND SECESSION

1852 Harriet Beecher Stowe's *Uncle Tom's Cabin* is published. The sentimental but powerful novel wins many new members for the antislavery cause.

1854 A coalition of antislavery politi-

cians from several parties forms a new group, the Republican Party, at a meeting in Ripon, Wisconsin.
•The Kansas-Nebraska Act is passed in May. Kansas and Nebraska are made into territories; the

legislature of each will decide whether or not to allow slavery, according popular sovereignty.

1855 Antislavery "free soilers" and proslavery settlers swarm into Kansas. Each side

A scene from Uncle Tom's Cabin

greatest good of the greatest number of people.

1860 Italian patriot Giuseppe Garibaldi begins his struggle to unite the states of Italy into one nation.

1861 Louis Pasteur, a French doctor, announces his theory that diseases are caused by

The landing of Garibaldi's troops at Marsala

invisible organisms called germs.
•Czar Alexander II grants freedom to Russia's serfs (peasants who by law and tradition have been "owned" by landowners).
•Italy is finally united under King Victor Emanuel II.

portrait studio in New York City.

1854 The Know-Nothing Party—a political movement opposed to immigration and the Roman Catholic Church—holds its first convention in New York City.

1857 Nearly 5,000 U.S. businesses fail following a financial "panic" in New York; widespread economic hardship results.
•After Mormon settlers in Utah attack a passing wagon train, President Buchanan orders troops sent to the area. The mostly bloodless "Mormon War" ends in June 1858.

1859 Edwin Drake sinks the first commercially successful oil well, in western Pennsylvania.

1860 The Pony Express begins; relays of riders carry mail from St. Joseph, Missouri, to Sacramento, California, in as little as six days.
•The population of the United States is 31.5 million.

1861 The first transcontinental telegraph line is completed, putting the Pony Express out of business.

hopes to gain enough votes to defeat the other on the slavery issue.

1856 Proslavery settlers destroy the town of Lawrence, headquarters of abolitionist activity in Kansas.
•The Kansas elections result in two governments, one antislavery and one proslavery. The conflict is marked by bloody violence.

1857 In May, the U.S. Supreme Court decides the case of *Dred Scott* v. *Sandford*. The court throws the case out, stating that, as a slave, Scott has no rights.

•Abraham Lincoln and Stephen Douglas, opponents in the Illinois senatorial race, meet in a series of debates. Lincoln opposes the extension of slavery in the West, while Douglas promotes popular sovereignty.

1859 Hoping to spark a slave revolt, abolitionists led by John Brown seize the federal arsenal at Harpers Ferry, Virginia. He is hanged.

THE PRESIDENTS OF THE UNITED STATES.

Part I
Conflict and Compromise

This print, showing the U.S. presidents from George Washington to James Polk, was published by Currier & Ives in 1844, the year Polk was elected. The signing of the Declaration of Independence is shown in the center. The patriotic and idealistic tone of the print does not reflect the turbulent political crises in the decades that preceded the Civil War.

The Civil War began on April 12, 1861, when Confederate cannons opened fire on Fort Sumter in the harbor at Charleston, South Carolina. The shots at Fort Sumter brought into flame a conflict that had been smoldering for decades.

The origins of the Civil War lie deep in America's history. Some historians say that the seeds of this war were sown in 1619, when the first African slaves arrived in the English colony of Jamestown, Virginia. Others give 1793, the year the cotton gin was invented, as the crucial date. This breakthrough helped turn the Southern states into a "cotton kingdom," which depended heavily on slavery to keep cotton production high. Still others stress the importance of the Mexican War of 1846–48, which won a huge stretch of Western land for the United States. This victory raised an important question— should slavery be permitted in the new territories of the West?

Other factors—economic differences, and the question of states' rights versus federal authority—helped lead the North and South to war. But the question of slavery was at the center of each controversy. How could a nation "conceived in Liberty, and dedicated to the proposition that all men are created equal," in Abraham Lincoln's words, exist with millions of its people in chains?

Throughout the first half of the nineteenth century, political compromises kept this question from splitting the nation in two. In 1820 and again in 1850, statesmen such as Henry Clay and Daniel Webster convinced Congress to accept temporary solutions to the slavery problem. But these acts soon proved to be flawed and short-lived. As the United States passed the mid-century mark, Americans in all parts of the country realized that a final showdown was approaching.

AMERICA IN 1820

As the United States entered the second decade of the nineteenth century, the nation celebrated what a Boston newspaper called "an era of good feelings." James Monroe (1758–1831) of Virginia had been re-elected as president with little opposition. The nation's independence, threatened during the War of 1812, was now secure. The bitter political debates of the early 1800s had given way to general agreement on most major issues. The nation's population, moving swiftly toward the 10-million mark, looked forward to years of peace, prosperity, and growth.

The United States in 1820 was very much a rural nation, although a revolution in transportation and industry was already under way. Three quarters of the population either farmed for a living or worked in a trade closely tied to agriculture. The nation's largest city, New York, was home to only 125,000 people. Except for Native Americans and almost 2 million black slaves, most Americans were native-born white Protestants of British ancestry. Only about 13,000 immigrants entered the United States in 1820. The great wave of immigration would not begin for another decade.

This peaceful, united nation was entering an era of change that would soon divide it in two. Such factors as immigration, industrialization, and political and economic changes all contributed to the split. But the root cause of the upcoming crisis was slavery. The first major conflict over the issue was already in progress as President Monroe began his second term.

James Monroe (1758–1831; above) was the last president who had fought in the Revolutionary War. He was a slave-owning Virginian, as were presidents Washington, Jefferson, and Madison.

Washington had been the nation's capital for only twenty years when James Monroe took office. This engraving (opposite, top) shows the view from the White House in 1820, looking down Pennsylvania Avenue toward the Capitol. Many of the city's buildings still bore scars from the British attack on the city during the War of 1812.

John Quincy Adams (1767–1848; right), Monroe's able secretary of state, was largely responsible for the Monroe Doctrine of 1823, the administration's best-known foreign policy statement. The son of second president John Adams (1753–1826), he later served one term (1825–29) as president himself.

THE ROOTS OF CONFLICT: SLAVERY

Slavery is defined as the ownership of one human being by another, allowing the owner to profit from the slave's forced labor. It has existed, in different forms, in many societies throughout history. But by the mid-1800s, the only areas in the Americas that practiced slavery were Brazil, Cuba, and the southern United States.

The first African slaves landed at the English colony of Jamestown in Virginia in 1619. Slavery existed in all of the original thirteen colonies, but it played a major economic role only in the South. After the Revolution, all states north of the Mason-Dixon line eventually freed their slaves.

Most of the leaders of the young United States opposed slavery, although several—including George Washington and Thomas Jefferson—owned slaves themselves. Most believed that slavery was economically inefficient as well as morally wrong. Competition from free labor, they hoped, would one day cause slavery to die out.

Then, in 1793, a Connecticut mechanic named Eli Whitney developed a machine called the cotton gin ("gin" was an old form of the word "engine"). By making the process of separating cotton fiber from the plant's seeds both easier and faster, the cotton gin transformed the economy of the South. Cotton soon became a major cash crop, and slave labor was used to grow and harvest it.

Tobacco was the South's chief export crop before the rise of the "Cotton Kingdom," and it remained an important crop in Virginia and in other border states. In this eighteenth-century engraving (above), slaves pack tobacco leaves in barrels, then roll the barrels into a drying shed where the leaves were cured (preserved) before being packed and shipped.

Slaves operate a cotton gin in this nineteenth-century wood-engraving (right). Capable of cleaning the seeds from fifty pounds of cotton per day, the gin allowed Southern planters to export about 150,000 pounds of cotton in 1800. Before the invention of the gin, the most cotton ever exported in a year was 18,000 pounds.

THE ROOTS OF CONFLICT: STATES' RIGHTS

In 1787, the Constitutional Convention met to establish an effective government for the thirteen states in the Union. Many of the delegates to the convention feared placing too much power in the hands of the national, or federal, government. For this reason, the Constitution made a distinction between the rights and responsibilities of the federal government and those of the individual state governments.

But the words of the Constitution meant different things to different people, and conflicts soon arose. The Federalist Party, strongest in the Northern states, supported the idea of a strong central government. The young nation's other major political party, the Democratic-Republicans, believed that the states had the right to nullify (declare invalid) federal laws they believed were unconstitutional.

As the eighteenth century ended and the nineteenth began, the Southern states increasingly protested what they saw as federal meddling in state affairs—usually over the issue of slavery. They feared that Washington was passing laws that favored the growing industrial economy of the North over the agricultural South. One example was the Tariff of 1828. It placed high duties (import taxes) on imported manufactured goods to protect factories in the North from foreign competition. Southern planters, however, favored lower-priced European goods, and the law came to be known as the "Tariff of Abominations" in the South.

Thomas Jefferson (1743–1826; above) supported states' rights and limited power for the federal government. (As president, however, he was happy to use his executive power to authorize the Louisiana Purchase.) Jefferson's views were opposed by Alexander Hamilton, the nation's first secretary of the treasury; Hamilton wanted a strong federal government, with states as "corporations for local purposes" only.

The Virginia and Kentucky Resolutions (right), written by Thomas Jefferson and James Madison in 1798, were a response to Congress's 1797 passage of the Alien and Sedition Acts, which partly restricted free speech. Later supporters of states' rights based their arguments on the principles of the Resolutions. This pamphlet containing the Resolutions was rushed into print in 1832 to support South Carolina's rejection of federal tariff laws.

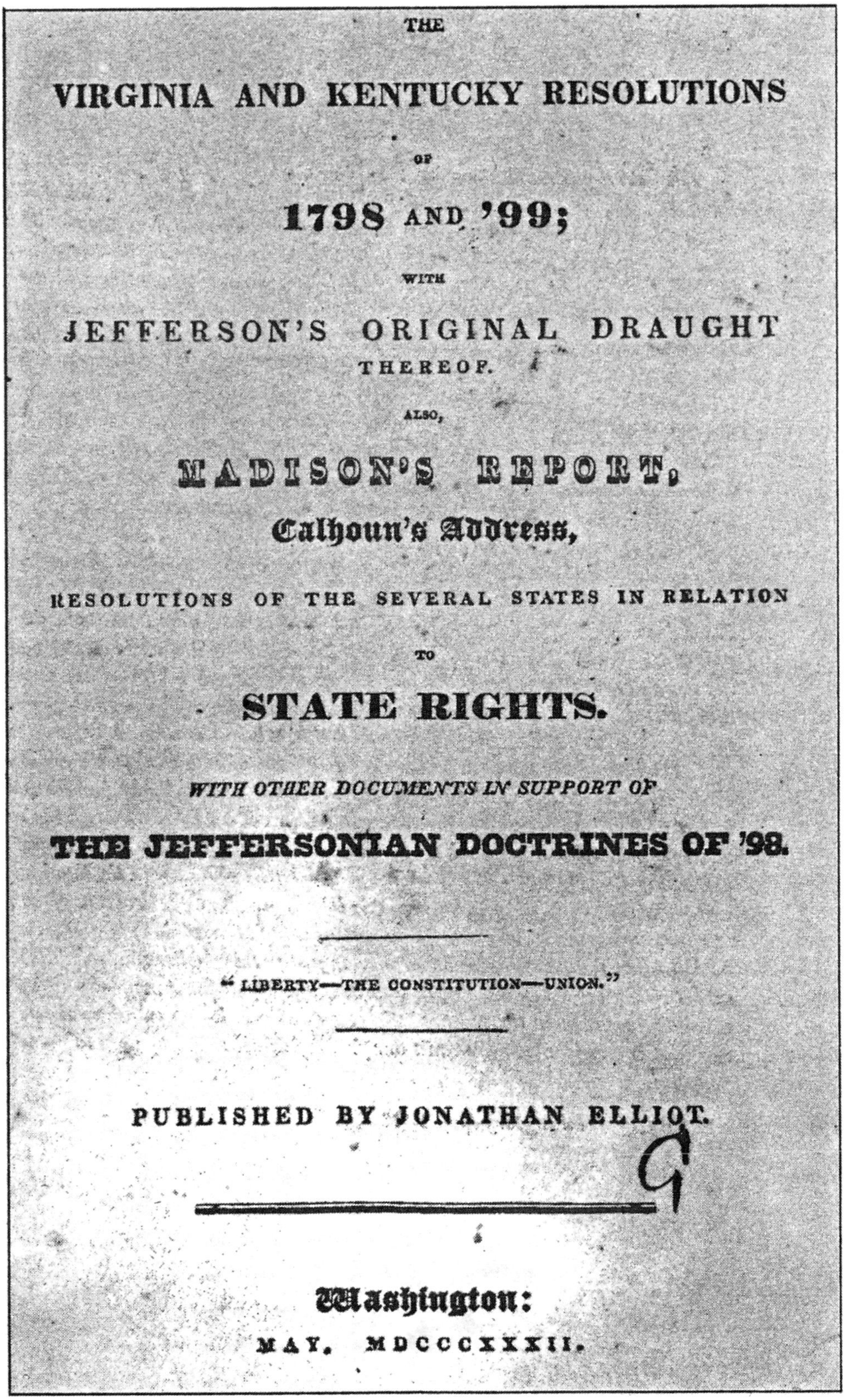

THE

VIRGINIA AND KENTUCKY RESOLUTIONS

OF

1798 AND '99;

WITH

JEFFERSON'S ORIGINAL DRAUGHT

THEREOF.

ALSO,

MADISON'S REPORT,

Calhoun's Address,

RESOLUTIONS OF THE SEVERAL STATES IN RELATION

TO

STATE RIGHTS.

WITH OTHER DOCUMENTS IN SUPPORT OF

THE JEFFERSONIAN DOCTRINES OF '98.

_____

" LIBERTY—THE CONSTITUTION—UNION."

_____

PUBLISHED BY JONATHAN ELLIOT.

_____

Washington:

MAY. MDCCCXXXII.

THE MISSOURI COMPROMISE

The Louisiana Purchase of 1803 nearly doubled the size of the United States. In 1817, the Missouri Territory—one of several territories organized from the purchase—asked to join the Union, with a state constitution permitting slavery. This would tip the balance of representation in Congress in favor of the slave-owning South, which many people in the North opposed.

With tensions running high in Congress, in the press, and in the public, Senator Henry Clay of Kentucky stepped in with a solution. The territory of Maine had asked for admission as a free state. With Maine in the Union as a free state, Missouri could be admitted as a slave state without upsetting the balance of power in the national government. To appease antislavery sentiment in the North, Clay's compromise plan also outlawed slavery in any new territories north of latitude 36' 30"—Missouri's southern border. In 1821, the bills, known together as the Missouri Compromise, passed into law. People everywhere rejoiced at the news, believing that the Compromise had permanently solved the problem of the expansion of slavery.

Others weren't so sure. Thomas Jefferson felt the new law signaled the beginning, not the end, of conflict. "I considered it the knell of the Union," he wrote. In the North, another aged statesman, John Adams, feared that the Compromise might be the title page "to a great, tragic volume."

A Virginian by birth but always identified with his adopted state of Kentucky, Henry Clay (above, top) devoted much of his career to keeping the different sections of the nation together. "I know no South, no North, no East, no West, to which I owe any allegiance," he said in one debate. "The Union, sir, is my country."

An English tourist described the eloquent and energetic Massachusetts senator Daniel Webster (above, bottom) as "a steam engine in trousers." On March 7, 1850, Webster gave a brilliant speech that won much support for the proposed compromise. It began: "I wish to speak today not as a Massachusetts man, not as a Northern man, but as an American."

This map shows how the Missouri Compromise divided the West. This region first stretched to what was then Spanish, and later Mexican, territory. When the United States gained this land as a result of the Mexican War, the bitter debate over slavery in the West began again.

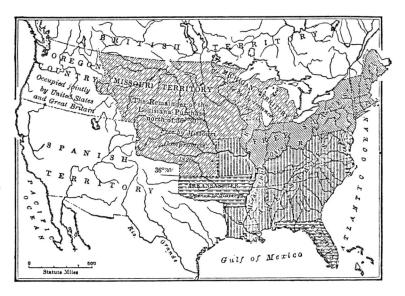

After several Northern congressmen voted against a bill limiting slavery in Missouri, Representative John Randolph of Virginia (shown here in a silhouette portrait) coined a new political label. He called the Northerners "doughfaces"—meaning that they could be molded, like dough, by Southern pressure.

THE INDUSTRIAL NORTH

The first half of the nineteenth century was a time of great economic change for the states north of the Ohio River. The Industrial Revolution, which first started in Great Britain in the 1790s, began to spread throughout New England. Textile mills sprang up to spin the cotton from the Southern states into fabric. Once the basis of the North's economy had moved from farming and fishing to industry, immigrants began pouring into cities such as New York and Boston. Spurred sometimes by the desire for political freedom, but more often by hunger and the hope of a better life, millions of people left Germany, Britain, Ireland, and other nations to try their luck in America.

They didn't always find prosperity. The North's economy suffered frequent "growing pains"—financial depressions—throughout the first half of the nineteenth century. And even when work was plentiful, conditions in the mills, shops, and factories were often harsh. Even for women and children, who made up a large part of the labor force, hours were long, wages low, and workplaces often unsafe. A worker who was laid off in bad times, or forced to work in brutal conditions, could do little to change his or her situation. Local governments were usually unwilling to regulate businesses and protect workers.

But unlike the slave of the South, the Northern worker, whether immigrant or native-born, was at least free—most importantly, free to move to the territories in the West.

New York surpassed Boston in population and commercial importance in the early nineteenth century. But Boston remained the nation's cultural capital, with many of the nation's greatest writers and thinkers— such as Ralph Waldo Emerson and Henry David Thoreau—living in or near the city. Shown here (right) is Beacon Hill in central Boston.

Investors provided the money that fueled the growing industrial economy of the North. By the middle of the nineteenth century, New York was the financial center of the nation as well as its largest city. This 1848 lithograph (below) shows the Merchant Exchange on Wall Street.

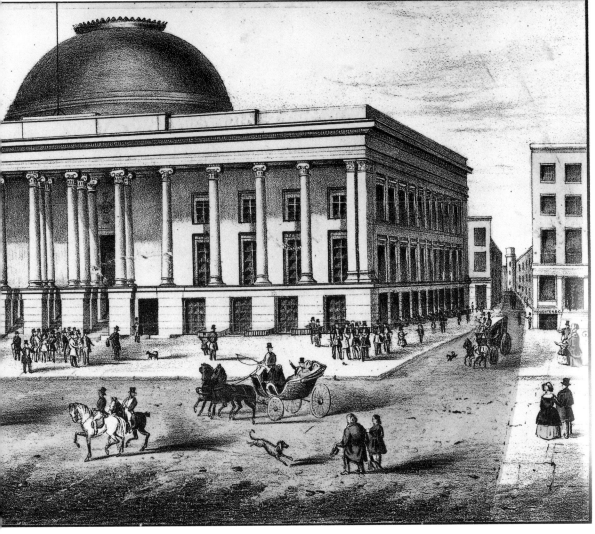

For many people in nine-teenth-century New England, the old pattern of farm life gave way to a new kind of life centered on the factory bell. In this engraving (right) based on a drawing by Winslow Homer, titled "Bell-Time," factory workers—young children among them—walk to work at a textile mill.

The Colt arms plant (below) was located in Hartford, Connecticut. Practically all of America's heavy industry was in the North—a fact that would give the North a major advantage when the Civil War finally began in 1861.

By 1836, almost nine out of ten "operatives" in the complex of textile mills at Lowell, Massachusetts, were young women. Shown here is the November 1845 edition of the Lowell Offering, a collection of poems and stories by "Factory Girl."

THE SOUTH: THE COTTON KINGDOM

The South's economy also changed greatly in the first decades of the nineteenth century. In the late 1700s, Southern states depended on exports of crops such as indigo, rice, and tobacco for cash. Cotton was a profitable crop, but difficult to cultivate because of the time-consuming task of separating the seeds from the fiber.

In 1793, Eli Whitney, a Connecticut schoolteacher on a visit to a Georgia farm, devised a simple machine that could easily separate cotton seed from fiber. Within decades, the invention made cotton the chief crop of the South and one of the nation's major products. By 1860, cotton accounted for more than half of all American exports. The "cotton kingdom" took deepest root in the new Southern states in the Mississippi Valley—Alabama, Mississippi, and Louisiana—but it was the mainstay of the entire region. Because of this dependence on cotton, the revolution in industry and transportation that swept the North didn't take hold in the South. Also, very few immigrants from Europe came to Southern ports.

At the beginning of the nineteenth century, many Southerners hoped that they would see slavery end in their lifetime; however, the invention of the cotton gin killed that hope. Now, cotton planting would require a large labor force, and in the South, labor meant slaves. By mid-century, public opinion in the South firmly supported slavery.

The Mississippi River provided a natural highway for transporting cotton to market at New Orleans, the South's chief port on the Gulf of Mexico. In this lithograph (right), slaves load cotton aboard a riverboat. Plantation owners were actually more likely to hire immigrant laborers for this job, because a valuable slave might be injured by a falling bale of cotton.

With a population of 150,000, New Orleans was the South's largest and most prosperous city. The Levee, the main commercial pier in New Orleans, is shown in this lithograph (below) by Currier & Ives. Cotton and other goods are waiting to be loaded onto the docked steamboats in the background.

The invention that transformed the South, the cotton gin, was largely the work of New Englander Eli Whitney (1765–1825; opposite). Whitney reportedly believed that the cotton gin would improve the lives of slaves by reducing the amount of work they had to do. In fact, it had the opposite effect.

This print (below) shows slave life on a cotton plantation. It depicts the sort of backbreaking labor involved in harvesting cotton. On most plantations, only a third of the slaves worked in the fields; the rest were house servants or crafts workers.

THE NULLIFICATION CONTROVERSY

In 1828, a pamphlet titled *The South Carolina Exposition and Protest* appeared. Its anonymous author argued that states had the right to nullify federal laws, such as the Tariff of 1828, which they considered unconstitutional. The author, John C. Calhoun of South Carolina, had to keep his identity secret. At the time, he was serving as vice president of the United States under President John Quincy Adams, a tariff supporter.

Because Calhoun supported Andrew Jackson in the presidential election of 1828, he kept the vice presidency for a second term. But when Jackson signed a second tariff act into law in 1832, Calhoun resigned.

In November 1832, South Carolina's state government passed a formal Ordinance of Nullification against the tariff. Some of the state's leaders proposed that South Carolina secede— leave the Union—rather than give in to Washington on the tariff issue.

President Jackson, newly elected for a second term, responded quickly and forcefully. On December 10, he declared that South Carolina had no right to disobey a federal law or to leave the Union. Soon after, Jackson sent warships into Charleston Harbor.

Four months later, South Carolina backed down. On March 2, 1833, Jackson signed a compromise tariff bill into law; two weeks later, South Carolina withdrew its ordinance. This controversy was the closest the nation had ever come to civil war.

John C. Calhoun (1782–1850; above) was secretary of war in the Monroe administration before serving as vice president under both John Quincy Adams and Andrew Jackson. After he left office, Andrew Jackson reportedly told a friend that one of the things he regretted not doing as president was "hanging John C. Calhoun."

This cartoon (below) gives the Southern view of the tariff controversy. The figure at right represents the North's industries, growing fat with federal protection from European competition. The starving figure at left, stooped under the weight of federal tariffs, symbolizes the South.

THE DIVIDED WEST

Between 1783 and 1848, the western boundary of the United States moved farther west in huge leaps, finally ending at the Pacific Ocean.

The states along the Great Lakes—Illinois, Indiana, Ohio, Michigan, and Wisconsin—were originally organized as the Northwest Territory in 1787. The Northwest Ordinance, the document that established this area's first government, prohibited slavery in the region. Many of its settlers came from New England and disliked slavery on principle. Also, because this region's economy was closely tied to the Northeastern states by a network of canals, roads, and railroads, it had no reason to depend on slavery.

West of the Mississippi River, in the vast areas gained by the Louisiana Purchase of 1803 and the Mexican War, the issue of slavery was more complicated. The Missouri Compromise of 1820 banned slavery in the West below latitude 36' 30". Most Western land was unsuitable for growing cotton and other slave-cultivated crops anyway. Even so, many Southerners had an interest in the region. If they were going to move to the West, they wanted to bring their slaves with them. They also hoped that the proposed transcontinental railroad would be built along a southern route, to give the South's economy a boost.

Many people in the North opposed Texas's admission to the Union. They feared that the huge territory would be broken up into several smaller states, giving the South greater power in Congress. In this woodcut (right), titled "Discussing the Texas Question," members of a political club listen as another member reads a pamphlet supporting the annexation of Texas.

This Currier & Ives lithograph (below), "The Pioneer's Home," depicts settlers returning to their cabin after a successful hunt. By 1860, half the nation's people lived west of the Appalachian Mountains, which had been the western edge of the frontier in colonial days.

THE MEXICAN WAR

The United States's war with Mexico (1846–48) ended in an American victory but helped set the stage for a far more costly conflict—the Civil War.

The immediate cause of the Mexican War was the former Mexican province of Texas. This area had attracted many American settlers in the early 1800s. In 1836, they rebelled against Mexican rule and established an independent republic. In 1845, Texas was annexed by the United States, and Mexico sent in troops to reclaim the land.

In early 1846, President James Polk ordered General Zachary Taylor to lead an army to the area located between the Nueces and Rio Grande rivers. When fighting between U.S. and Mexican troops broke out in May, Congress quickly declared war. In the summer and fall of 1846, Taylor's troops won a string of victories in northern Mexico. At the same time, American forces captured California and New Mexico.

In March 1847, a second American army under General Winfield Scott landed near the Mexican port of Veracruz. Scott's outnumbered army marched through central Mexico. The nation's capital, Mexico City, fell to the Americans on September 13.

The Treaty of Guadalupe Hidalgo, signed in February 1848, ended the war. Under its terms, the United States gained almost 500 million square miles of Mexican land. Supporters of Manifest Destiny—the idea that the United States should expand to the Pacific—saw their dream fulfilled. But this victory raised the issue of slavery in the West once again.

Most historians believe President James K. Polk (1795–1849; right) hoped to trigger a clash with Mexico in order to seize California and Mexico's other southwestern territories. The Polk administration had previously tried to buy California from Mexico, without success.

One of the toughest battles waged by General Zachary Taylor's army in northern Mexico was for the key city of Monterrey. Mexican troops held the high ground around the city. It took a fierce uphill assault to dislodge them, as shown in this lithograph (below), before the town itself could be captured.

Shown in this illustration (above) is the storming of Chapultepec
Castle outside Mexico City on September 13, 1848. Among the
attackers was young Lieutenant Ulysses S. Grant; the soldier who
finally ran the U.S. flag up over the fortress was George Pickett,
who would later help lead a famous charge at the Battle of Get-
tysburg in 1863.

A Mexican War hero, Virginia-born General Zachary Taylor
(1784–1850), at left in this campaign poster (opposite, top), was
the Whig presidential candidate in the 1848 election. Taylor easily
beat his Democratic rival, Lewis Cass of Michigan, but died after
sixteen months in office. Vice President Millard Fillmore, at Taylor's right in the poster, succeeded him in July 1850.

In this lithograph (right), American dragoons—heavily armed cavalry—fight their way through a Mexican ambush. (American soldiers did not, however, fight in the gaudy dress uniforms shown
here.) Disease killed more soldiers than Mexican bullets during
the war; only about 1,700 Americans died in combat, while
almost 12,000 were felled by illness.

THE CRISIS OVER CALIFORNIA

CALIFORNIA REPUBLIC

Arguments over slavery in the former Mexican lands began even before the war's end. In late 1846, President Polk asked Congress for $2 million to open peace negotiations with Mexico. Pennsylvania representative David Wilmot (1814–68) asked for an amendment to the proposed bill that would forbid slavery in any territory won from Mexico. The bill eventually passed without this "Wilmot Proviso."

The huge territory that the United States gained from the Treaty of Guadalupe Hidalgo would eventually become six states, including California. Most of this "Mexican Cession," however, was sparsely populated. It would be years before most portions of this land would be ready for statehood. Many Americans believed slavery was not an issue that needed to be solved immediately in the West.

Then, in March 1848, gold was discovered in California. During the following year, 80,000 fortune-seeking Americans arrived there, creating a desperate need for an organized government. In October 1849, leading Californians met at Monterey, drafted a constitution forbidding slavery, and petitioned Congress for statehood.

Southern politicians immediately rose in opposition. Oregon had been admitted as a free state in August with the understanding that the next Western territory to join the Union would allow slavery. But Zachary Taylor, now president, supported California's admission as a free state. The nation faced its gravest political crisis since the controversy over Missouri.

On June 14, 1846, when this flag (above) was raised over the fortress at Sonoma, California was declared the "Bear Flag Republic." The Americans who hoisted the flag announced that California was now independent from Mexico, and they quickly voted to join the United States.

Much of the land around Sacramento was owned by John Sutter, a Swiss immigrant. On January 24, 1848, a mechanic named John Marshall discovered gold near one of Sutter's sawmills, sparking the great "Gold Rush" that led to statehood for California. This wood-engraving (opposite, top) shows California miners using one of many different methods for finding gold.

This lithograph (right) shows the town of Sacramento, at the junction of the Sacramento and American rivers, in 1850. The discovery of gold at nearby Coloma quickly swelled Sacramento's population and increased its importance, as shown by the many ships arriving at the town's waterfront. In 1854, Sacramento became California's state capital.

THE COMPROMISE OF 1850

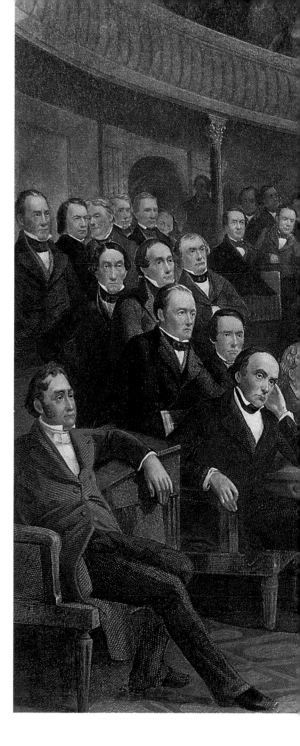

The 1849–50 controversy over California echoed the 1819–20 crisis over Missouri. Once again, the root of the disagreement between North and South was a struggle for political power. Of the thirty states in the Union, fifteen were free and fifteen slave. If California were admitted as a free state, the balance of power in the Senate would swing to the North.

The South's aging champion, Senator John C. Calhoun, fought to prevent this outcome and bitterly opposed any compromise over the issue. But after Calhoun died in March 1850, more moderate voices were heard.

Just as he had in 1820, Senator Henry Clay of Kentucky rose to offer a compromise. Clay proposed not one law but several separate measures. Together, he hoped they would not only settle the issue of California, but end the debate over slavery forever.

Clay's Omnibus Compromise Bill, later known as the Compromise of 1850, called for California's admission as a free state. At the same time, it allowed citizens of the newly organized New Mexico and Utah territories to decide for themselves whether to permit or outlaw slavery. The slave trade would be prohibited in Washington, D.C. In order to win Southern support, the bill also strengthened the Fugitive Slave Act of 1793.

With support from prominent Northern politicians, Clay's compromise passed Congress and became law on September 20, 1850.

The Compromise of 1850 was the last great act of Henry Clay's political career; he died two years after its passage. It took all Clay's skill, plus those of Daniel Webster and newer figures such as Illinois Senator Stephen Douglas, to win Congressional approval for the plan.

THE FUGITIVE SLAVE ACT

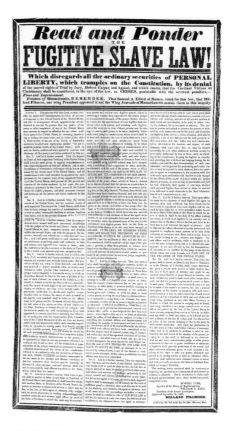

In the North, the most controversial part of the Compromise of 1850 was the changes to the Fugitive Slave Act. Slaveowners had always had the right, in theory, to pursue runaway slaves in free states and territories. Police and other authorities, however, often refused to cooperate. The new, stricter law required local authorities to help Southern masters (or the professional slave catchers they hired) to capture and return slaves who had escaped to freedom in the North. It also gave federal officials the power to hand over runaways to their masters.

The new Fugitive Slave Act included even harsher measures. Suspected runaways had no right to a trial if their status was questioned. Also, a white person who hid a runaway slave or helped one escape could be sent to prison for up to six months.

In protest, several Northern states passed "personal liberty laws," which outlawed the return of escaped slaves against their will. In 1859, however, the Supreme Court ruled such laws unconstitutional.

The Act was put to the test in the streets and fields as well as in the courtroom. Abolitionists—antislavery activists—led raids on jails to free captured slaves. In one 1851 incident, free blacks and abolitionists fired on slave catchers at Christiana, Pennsylvania, killing one man and wounding several others. Southerners pointed to these incidents and claimed that the North was not holding up its part of the Compromise of 1850.

This broadside (above) against the Fugitive Slave Act was printed in Massachusetts, the stronghold of antislavery feeling. The Act met with outrage among many abolitionist intellectuals. Author Ralph Waldo Emerson (1803–82) called it a "filthy enactment" and urged citizens not to obey it.

The most notorious incident caused by the Fugitive Slave Act occurred in May 1854, when a federal marshall arrested escaped slave Anthony Burns in Boston. After an antislavery mob tried to free Burns from jail, U.S. Marines returned him to his master. Shown here (opposite, top) is a portrait of Burns, surrounded by scenes from his capture.

This cartoon (right) criticizes those Northern politicians and abolitionists who urged authorities to appeal to a "higher law" by not enforcing the Fugitive Slave Act. The cartoon's title, "What's Sauce for the Goose is Sauce for the Gander," expresses the Southern belief that the North wasn't obeying of the Compromise of 1850.

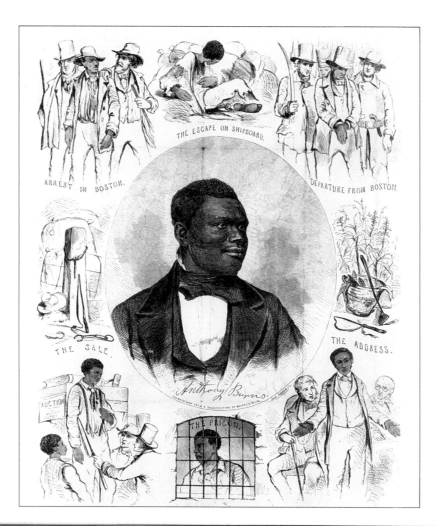

THE ESCAPE ON SHIPBOARD.

ARREST IN BOSTON.

DEPARTURE FROM BOSTON.

THE SALE.

THE ADDRESS.

THE PRISON.

Anthony Burns.

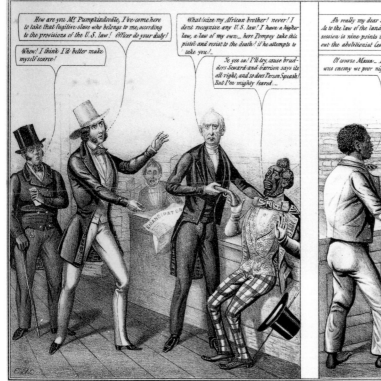

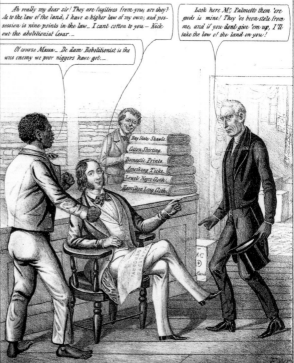

SUPPORTERS OF SLAVERY

Up until the early nineteenth century, most leading Americans viewed slavery as a necessary evil at best. Even many Southern slaveholders believed that the institution would die off because of competition from free farmers and laborers.

The violence that resulted from several slave revolts, however, made Southern whites worry about what would happen if hundreds of thousands of slaves were suddenly freed. Would they seek revenge against their former masters? Thomas Jefferson had compared slavery to holding a wolf by the ears: It was dangerous, but letting go might be disastrous.

After slave-grown cotton became the South's economic mainstay, a new attitude toward slavery emerged. Many Southerners now believed slavery was a good thing for blacks and whites alike. Planters began to refer to slavery as the South's "peculiar institution." These supporters of slavery pointed out that slaves (at least in theory) were cared for from cradle to grave, unlike the North's factory workers. Besides, they said, slavery had always existed. Southern writers used the Bible and Greek and Roman history to claim that slavery was the foundation of many great societies.

Despite these arguments, the main reason for the South's defense of slavery was simple economics. By 1860, the total worth of the South's slaves was over $2 billion. The South could not hope to stay on equal footing with the prosperous North and West without the labor that slaves provided.

After the uprising led by Virginia slave Nat Turner in August 1831, Virginia and other Southern states passed strict "black codes," restricting the movements and activities of slaves and free blacks. In many places it became illegal to teach slaves to read. This dramatic, although inaccurate, woodcut (opposite) shows scenes from the rebellion.

This cartoon (below) uses a favorite tactic of the supporters of slavery: It contrasts the conditions of Southern slaves with those of industrial workers—in this case, in England. The left panel shows well-fed, contented slaves at rest; the right panel depicts sick, exhausted factory hands.

THE REALITY OF SLAVERY

Imagine that you were someone else's property. Imagine that because of the color of your skin, you could be bought and sold, even if that meant never seeing your friends, parents, or children again. Imagine that you were forced to work hard, but gained nothing from your work. Imagine not being able to learn to read, to travel freely, or even to leave your home. And imagine that if you disobeyed any of the many rules that governed your life, you faced severe punishment—including beating or whipping.

This was the reality for slaves in the American South. There were 4 million slaves in the United States in 1860, making up about 12 percent of the nation's population of 31.4 million. A slave might live his or her life on a single plantation, or be bought and sold many times. In 1860, a "field hand"—a strong slave trained for outdoor work—sold for up to $1,800. Women usually sold for about half the price of men; children (who often began working full-time at age ten) for even less.

Despite slavery's importance to the South, there were few truly large plantations: In 1850, only 8,000 Southerners owned more than fifty slaves. Most slaves belonged to smaller plantations. But whether a slave lived on a huge Mississippi cotton plantation or a small Virginia tobacco farm, he or she was still a person without rights—and without freedom.

Most owners didn't mistreat their slaves—a slave was, after all, considered valuable property. But some ordered brutal punishments—including whipping and branding with hot irons—for even the most minor "crimes," such as accidentally breaking tools. This photograph (above) shows a Louisiana slave, bound by chains and a restraining "choker" around his neck, who has just been branded by his master.

Some slaves were freed by their masters, and a few managed to buy their freedom. But for most slaves, the only way out of bondage was to escape to one of the free states. Escaped slaves, however, were never truly safe: Masters often hired slave catchers to kidnap and return fugitives, as shown in this woodcut.

THE ABOLITIONISTS

Opposition to slavery began in colonial times. The first book protesting it, *The Selling of Joseph* by Samuel Sewall, was published in 1700. Even earlier, the Quakers and other religious groups denounced slavery and outlawed it among their members.

In the early nineteenth century, a new breed of outspoken antislavery activists appeared. They were known as abolitionists, for their desire to abolish slavery in the United States. They included free blacks, escaped slaves, and whites. Most were from the North, especially New England, but not all. Two well-known abolitionists were sisters Sarah and Angelina Grimké, who saw the evils of slavery firsthand while growing up on a plantation in South Carolina.

The most famous abolitionist was William Lloyd Garrison of Massachusetts. In 1831, Garrison founded a newspaper, *The Liberator*, which served as the voice of the movement. Garrison also helped establish the American Anti-Slavery Society, the largest abolitionist organization, in 1833.

While many Northerners were opposed to extending slavery into the West, most were willing to accept slavery in the South, where it had existed for centuries. The abolitionists, however, demanded an end to slavery everywhere, and they did everything possible to keep the issue in the public eye. Garrison, for example, publicly burned a copy of the Constitution, calling the document "a covenant with hell" because it accepted slavery.

William Lloyd Garrison (1805–79; above) was an outspoken opponent of slavery who offended some Northerners. Even Ralph Waldo Emerson, a fierce foe of slavery, advised Garrison and his followers to be more moderate. They should, he said, "Love their black brethren a little less, and their neighbors a little more."

Abolitionist organizations turned out scores of publications, including this almanac (opposite, top), published by the American Anti-Slavery Society in 1840. The cover illustration protests a New York State law requiring blacks to live in the state for nine months before claiming residency. This meant that recently escaped slaves couldn't claim protection from slave catchers.

Shown here (right) is the masthead of The Liberator, *Garrison's abolitionist newspaper. At its founding, Garrison outlined his, and the paper's, attitude toward slavery: "I will be as harsh as truth and as uncompromising as justice . . . AND I WILL BE HEARD."*

THE AMERICAN ANTI-SLAVERY ALMANAC,

FOR

1840,

BEING BISSEXTILE OR LEAP-YEAR, AND THE 64TH OF AMERICAN
INDEPENDENCE. CALCULATED FOR NEW YORK; ADAPTED
TO THE NORTHERN AND MIDDLE STATES.

NORTHERN HOSPITALITY—NEW YORK NINE MONTHS' LAW.
The slave steps out of the slave-state, and his chains fall. A free state, with another chain, stands ready to re-enslave him.

Thus saith the Lord, Deliver him that is spoiled out of the hands of the oppressor.

NEW YORK:
PUBLISHED BY THE AMERICAN ANTI-SLAVERY SOCIETY,
NO. 143 NASSAU STREET.

He that STEALETH a man, and SELLETH him, or if he be found in his hand, he shall surely be put to death. *Ex.* xxi. 16.

Thou shalt not deliver unto his master the servant which is escaped from his master unto thee: He shall dwell with thee, *even* among you, in that place which he shall choose, in one of thy gates where it liketh him best: thou shalt not OPPRESS him.—*Deut.* xxiii. 15, 16.

And if a man smite the eye of his servant, or the eye of his maid, that it perish, he shall let him go free for his eye's sake. And if he smite out his man-servant's tooth, or his maid-servant's tooth; he shall let him go free for his tooth's sake.—*Ex.* xxi. 26, 27.

If a man be just, and do that which is lawful and right; hath not oppressed any; hath spoiled none by violence; hath executed true judgment between man and man, he shall surely live.—*Ezekiel* xviii. 5—9.

Thou shalt tread upon the lion and adder; the young lion and the dragon shalt thou trample under feet.

Is not this the fast that I have chosen? to loose the bands of wickedness, to undo the heavy burdens, to let the OPPRESSED go FREE, and that ye break every yoke.—*Isaiah* lviii. 6.

Ye tithe mint, and anise, and cummin, and all manner of herbs, and pass over the weightier matters of the law, judgment, mercy, and faith: these ought ye to have done, and not leave the other undone.—*Matthew* xxiii. 23.

Thus man devotes his fellow man—
Chains him, and tasks him, and exacts his sweat,
With stripes, that mercy with a bleeding heart,
Weeps when she sees inflicted on a beast.
I would not have a slave to till my ground,
To carry me, to fan me while I sleep,
And tremble when I wake, for all the wealth
That sinews bought and sold have ever earn'd.
No; dear as freedom is,—
I had much rather be myself the slave,
And wear the bonds, than fasten them on him. *Cowper.*

DECLARATION OF THE ANTI-SLAVERY CONVENTION.

ASSEMBLED IN PHILADELPHIA, DECEMBER 4, 1833.

THE Convention assembled in the city of Philadelphia to organize a National Anti-Slavery Society, promptly seize the opportunity to promulgate the following DECLARATION OF SENTIMENTS, as cherished by them in relation to the enslavement of one-sixth portion of the American people.

More than fifty-seven years have elapsed since a band of patriots convened in this place, to devise measures for the deliverance of this country from a foreign yoke. The corner-stone upon which they founded the TEMPLE OF FREEDOM was broadly this—"that all men are created equal; that they are endowed by their Creator with certain inalienable rights; that among these are life, LIBERTY, and the pursuit of happiness." At the sound of their trumpet-call, three millions of people rose up as from the sleep of death, and rushed to the strife of blood; deeming it more glorious to die instantly as freemen, than desirable to live one hour as slaves. They were few in number—poor in resources; but the honest conviction that TRUTH, JUSTICE, and RIGHT were on their side, made them invincible.

We have met together for the achievement of an enterprise, without which, that of our fathers is incomplete; and which, for its magnitude, solemnity, and probable results upon the destiny of the world, as far transcends theirs, as moral truth does physical force.

In purity of motive, in earnestness of zeal, in decision of purpose, in intrepidity of action, in steadfastness of faith, in sincerity of spirit, we would not be inferior to them.

Their principles led them to wage war against their oppressors, and to spill human blood like water, in order to be free. *Ours* forbid the doing of evil that good may come, and lead us to reject, and to entreat the oppressed to reject, the use of all carnal weapons for deliverance from bondage; relying solely upon those which are spiritual, and mighty through God to the pulling down of strong holds.

Their measures were physical resistance—the marshalling in arms—the hostile array—the mortal encounter. *Ours* shall be such only as the opposition of moral purity to moral corruption—the destruction of error by the potency of truth—the overthrow of prejudice by the power of love—and the abolition of slavery by the spirit of repentance.

Their grievances, great as they were, were trifling in comparison with the wrongs and sufferings of those for whom we plead. Our fathers were never slaves—never bought and sold like cattle—never shut out from the light of knowledge and religion—never subjected to the lash of brutal task-masters.

But those, for whose emancipation we are striving—constituting at the present time at least one-sixth part of our countrymen,—are recognised by the law, and treated by their fellow-beings, as marketable commodities—as goods and chattels—as brute beasts; are plundered daily of the fruits of their toil without redress; really enjoying no constitutional nor legal protection from licentious and murderous outrages upon their persons; are ruthlessly torn asunder—the tender babe from the arms of its frantic mother—the heart-broken wife from her weeping husband—at the caprice or pleasure of irresponsible tyrants. For the crime of having a dark complexion, they suffer the pangs of hunger, the infliction of stripes, and the ignominy of brutal servitude. They are kept in heathenish darkness by laws expressly enacted to make their instruction a criminal offence.

These are the prominent circumstances in the condition of more than two millions of our people, the proof of which may be found in thousands of indisputable facts, and in the laws of the slave-holding States.

Hence we maintain—That in view of the civil and religious privileges of this nation, the guilt of its oppression is unequalled by any other on the face of the earth; and, therefore, that it is bound to repent instantly, to undo the heavy burden, to break every yoke, and to let the oppressed go free.

We further maintain—That no man has a right to enslave or imbrute his brother—to hold or acknowledge him, for one moment, as a piece of merchandise—to keep back his hire by fraud—or to brutalize his mind by denying him the means of intellectual, social, and moral improvement.

The right to enjoy liberty is inalienable. To invade it, is to usurp the prerogative of JEHOVAH. Every man has a right to his own body—to the products of his own labour—to the protection of law—and to the common advantages of society. It is piracy to buy or steal a native African, and subject him to servitude. Surely the sin is as great to enslave an AMERICAN as an AFRICAN.

Therefore we believe and affirm—That there is no difference, *in principle*, between the African slave trade and American slavery—That every American citizen, who retains a human being in involuntary bondage, as his property, is [according to Scripture*] a MAN STEALER—That the slaves ought instantly to be set free, and brought under the protection of law—That if they had lived from the time of Pharaoh down to the present period, and had been entailed through successive generations, their right to be free could never have been alienated, but their claims would have constantly risen in solemnity—That all those laws which are now in force, admitting the right of slavery, are therefore before God utterly null and void; being an audacious usurpation of the Divine prerogative, a daring infringement on the law of Nature, a base overthrow of the very foundations of the social compact, a complete extinction of all the relations, endearments, and obligations of mankind, and a presumptuous transgression of all the holy commandments—and that therefore they ought to be instantly abrogated.

We further believe and affirm—That all persons of colour who possess the qualifications which are demanded of others, ought to be admitted forthwith to the enjoyment of the same privileges, and the exercise of the same prerogatives, as others—That the paths of preferment, of wealth, and of intelligence, should be opened as widely to them as to persons of a white complexion.

We maintain that no compensation should be given to the planters emancipating their slaves—Because it would be a surrender of the great fundamental principle, that man cannot hold property in man—Because SLAVERY IS A CRIME, AND THEREFORE IT IS NOT AN ARTICLE TO BE SOLD—Because the holders of slaves are not the just proprietors of what they claim; freeing the slaves is not depriving them of property, but restoring it to its right owners; it is not wronging the master, but righting the slave—restoring him to himself—Because immediate and general emancipation would only destroy nominal, not real property; it would not amputate a limb or break a bone of the slaves, but by infusing motives into their breasts would make them doubly valuable to the masters as free labourers; and, because, if compensation is to be given at all, it should be given to the outraged and guiltless slaves, and not to those who have plundered and abused them.

We regard, as delusive, cruel, and dangerous, any scheme of expatriation which pretends to aid, either directly or indirectly, in the emancipation of the slaves, or to be a substitute for the immediate and total abolition of slavery.

We fully and unanimously recognise the sovereignty of each State, to legislate exclusively on the subject of slavery which is tolerated within its limits; we concede that Congress, *under the present national compact*, has no right to interfere with any of the slave States, in relation to this momentous subject.

But we maintain that Congress has a right, and is solemnly bound to suppress the domestic slave trade between the several States, and to abolish slavery in those portions of our territory which the Constitution has placed under its exclusive jurisdiction.

We also maintain that there are, at the present time, the highest obligations resting upon the people of the free States, to remove slavery by moral and political action, as prescribed in the Constitution of the United States. They are now living under a pledge of their tremendous physical force to fasten the galling fetters of tyranny upon the limbs of millions in the Southern States; they are liable to be called at any moment to suppress a general insurrection of the slaves: they authorize the slave owner to vote for three-fifths of his slaves as property, and thus enable him to perpetuate his oppression; they support a standing army at the South for its protection; and they seize the slave who has escaped into their territories, and send him back to be tortured by an enraged master or a brutal driver. This relation to slavery is criminal and full of danger: IT MUST BE BROKEN UP.

These are our views and principles—these, our designs and measures. With entire confidence in the over-ruling justice of God, we plant ourselves upon the Declaration of our Independence and the truths of Divine Revelation as upon the EVERLASTING ROCK.

We shall organize Anti-Slavery Societies, if possible, in every city, town, and village in our land.

We shall send forth Agents to lift up the voice of remonstrance, of warning, of entreaty, and of rebuke.

We shall circulate, unsparingly and extensively, anti-slavery tracts and periodicals.

We shall enlist the pulpit and the press in the cause of the suffering and the dumb.

We shall aim at a purification of the churches from all participation in the guilt of slavery.

We shall encourage the labour of freemen rather than that of the slaves, by giving a preference to their productions: and

We shall spare no exertions nor means to bring the whole nation to a speedy repentance.

Our trust for victory is solely in GOD. *We* may be personally defeated, but our principles never. TRUTH, JUSTICE, REASON, HUMANITY, must and will gloriously triumph. Already a host is coming up to the help of the Lord against the mighty, and the prospect before us is full of encouragement.

Submitting this DECLARATION to the candid examination of the people of this country, and of the friends of liberty throughout the world, we hereby affix our signatures to it; pledging ourselves that, under the guidance and by the help of Almighty God, we will do all that in us lies, consistently with this Declaration of our principles, to overthrow the most execrable system of slavery, that has ever been witnessed upon earth—to deliver our land from its deadliest curse—to wipe out the foulest stain which rests upon our national escutcheon—and to secure to the coloured population of the United States all the rights and privileges which belong to them as men, and as Americans—come what may to our persons, our interests, or our reputations—whether we live to witness the triumph of LIBERTY, JUSTICE, and HUMANITY, or perish ultimately as martyrs in this great, benevolent, and holy cause. Done in Philadelphia, this Sixth day of December, A. D. 1833.

*Exodus xxi. 16—Deuteronomy xxiv. 7.

Maine.
DAVID THURSTON,
NATHAN WINSLOW,
JOSEPH SOUTHWICK,
JAMES FREDERIC OTIS,
ISAAC WINSLOW.

New Hampshire.
DAVID CAMPBELL.

Vermont.
ORSON S. MURRAY.

Massachusetts.
DANIEL S. SOUTHMAYD,
EFFINGHAM L. CAPRON,
JOSHUA COFFIN,
AMOS A. PHELPS,
JOHN G. WHITTIER,
HORACE P. WAKEFIELD,
JAMES G. BARBADOES,
DAVID T. KIMBALL, JR.
DANIEL E. JEWETT,
JOHN R. CAMBELL,
NATHANIEL SOUTHARD,
ARNOLD BUFFUM,
WILLIAM L. GARRISON.

Rhode Island.
JOHN PRENTICE,
GEORGE W. BENSON,
RAY POTTER.

Connecticut.
SAMUEL J. MAY,
ALPHEUS KINGSLEY,
EDWIN A. STILLMAN,
SIMEON S JOCELYN,
ROBERT B. HALL.

New York.
BERIAH GREEN, JR.
LEWIS TAPPAN,
JOHN RANKIN,
WILLIAM GREEN, JR.
ABRAAM L. COX,
WILLIAM GOODELL,
ELIZUR WRIGHT, JR.
CHARLES W. DENISON,
JOHN FROST.

New Jersey.
JONATHAN PARKHURST,
CHALKLEY GILLINGHAM,
JOHN McCULLOUGH,
JAMES WHITE.

Pennsylvania.
EVAN LEWIS,
EDWIN A. ATLEE,
ROBERT PURVIS,
JAS. McCRUMMILL,
THOMAS SHIPLEY,
BARTH'W FUSSELL,
DAVID JONES,
ENOCH MACK,
JAMES McKIM,
AARON VICKERS,
JAMES LOUGHEAD,
EDWIN P. ATLEE,
THOMAS WHITSON,
JOHN R. SLEEPER,
JOHN SHARP, JR.
JAMES MOTT.

Ohio.
JOHN M. STERLING,
MILTON SUTLIFF,
LEVI SUTLIFF.

MERRIHEW & GUNN, Printers, *No. 7 Carter's Alley.*

The American Anti-Slavery Society was organized in 1833 in Philadelphia, when this declaration of principles (opposite) was signed. Among the signers were such famous abolitionists as William Lloyd Garrison, Lewis Tappan, and Robert Purvis, one of the chief "conductors" of the Underground Railroad.

This engraving (below) shows Bostonians—including free blacks—listening to an abolitionist speaker on Boston Common. Many Northerners, especially immigrants who feared economic competition from blacks, hated the abolitionists. In September 1835, a Boston mob threw a rope around William Lloyd Garrison and dragged him through the streets.

AN ERA OF REFORM

Abolitionism was only one of many reform movements sweeping the country in the first half of the nineteenth century. New ideas seemed to spring up naturally in what was still a young nation.

Many of these movements had their roots in the Second Great Awakening, a religious revival that swept the nation in the early 1800s. At the same time, several new religious movements began. The most successful of these was the Church of Latter-Day Saints, or Mormons, founded in western New York State in 1830 by Joseph Smith.

Economic changes also led to social experiments. In response to the rise of industry, several "utopian" communities sprang up. These communities, usually short-lived, prohibited private property, government, and sometimes even marriage so that members could live in "true equality." One of the best-known was New Harmony, Indiana, founded in 1825 by English philosopher Robert Owen.

Many American women, too, were eager for reform. At this time, women still did not have the right to vote. They had few legal rights in most states, and some states would not even allow women to own property. In 1848, a group of women and men met at Seneca Falls, New York, in Elizabeth Cady Stanton's home. They drafted a "Declaration of Sentiments," calling for equal treatment of men and women, including women's suffrage (the right to vote). The Seneca Falls convention marked the beginning of the American women's rights movement.

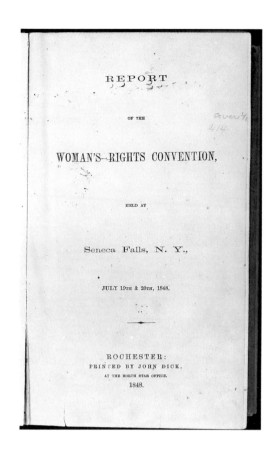

Many of the people involved in the struggle against slavery were also active in the cause of women's rights. This report (above) on the Seneca Falls convention, for example, was prepared at the office of the North Star, *an abolitionist newspaper edited by former slave Frederick Douglass.*

Not everyone liked the new trends in American society. Some people, in both the North and South, felt threatened by the many immigrants arriving in the country. Opponents of immigration formed a political party, called the "Know-Nothings." This engraving (opposite, top) from a London newspaper shows a Know-Nothing rally in New York City in the 1850s.

Organized labor was another reform movement that gathered strength in the years before the Civil War. In this illustration (opposite, bottom), female workers from a shoe factory in Lynn, Massachusetts, march during a strike for higher wages in 1860. They carry a banner proclaiming that they will "not be slaves."

UNCLE TOM'S CABIN

Abolitionists published newspapers, magazines, petitions, and pamphlets—all denouncing slavery. There was so much antislavery literature that several Southern states banned it from the mail. But none of these publications stirred up as much opposition to slavery as one novel: *Uncle Tom's Cabin*, by Harriet Beecher Stowe.

A native of Connecticut, Stowe was the daughter of Lyman Beecher, a famous Congregationalist minister. While living in Ohio, she visited a plantation in Kentucky. Shocked by what she saw of slavery, and further enraged by the Fugitive Slave Act of 1850, Stowe poured her emotions into a novel. It told the story of Uncle Tom, a saintly slave who is beaten to death for refusing to reveal the hiding place of two escaped slaves.

First serialized in an antislavery newspaper in 1851, *Uncle Tom's Cabin* appeared in book form a year later and caused an immediate sensation. The book sold a record-breaking 300,000 copies within a few months.

To modern readers, *Uncle Tom's Cabin* seems sentimental and unrealistic. But Stowe's portrayal of black characters as real people with real emotions was a breakthrough. Many of the people who read the book became converts to the antislavery movement. Southerners were disturbed by the popularity of *Uncle Tom's Cabin*, and several Southern writers collaborated on a book, *The Pro-Slavery Argument*, written to counter Stowe's portrayal of slave life.

When Harriet Beecher Stowe (1811–96; above) visited President Abraham Lincoln in 1863, he reportedly said to the short, frail-looking author, "So you're the little woman who wrote the book that made this great war." Lincoln borrowed Uncle Tom's Cabin *from the Library of Congress in 1862, as he prepared to issue the Emancipation Proclamation.*

In this engraving (opposite, top) from an illustrated edition of Uncle Tom's Cabin, *planter George Shelby frees his slaves, who respond joyfully to the news. While Stowe's book was deeply critical of the South, its chief villain, the cruel overseer Simon Legree, was a Northerner.*

This playbill (opposite, bottom) advertises one of the many stage adaptations of Uncle Tom's Cabin. *Plays based on the book continued to draw audiences for decades after the Civil War. As time went on, however, these productions often turned into vaudeville shows with little or no relation to Stowe's novel.*

For President

ABRAM LINCOLN.

For Vice President

HANNIBAL HAMLIN.

This Republican campaign flag from the election of 1860 misspells Lincoln's first name as "Abram." His running mate, Hannibal Hamlin of Maine, had an unusually dark complexion; Southern Democrats claimed that he was actually a black man.

The decade between 1851 and 1861 was one of the most turbulent decades in the history of the United States—and by the end of this period, the nation would be split in two.

By the early 1850s, the Missouri Compromise, once hailed as a permanent solution to the slavery issue, could no longer ease the tension between North and South. The Compromise of 1850 helped, but only briefly. In the words of Ohio senator Salmon Chase, "The question of slavery . . . has been avoided. It has not been settled."

The Kansas-Nebraska Act of 1854, followed by the Dred Scott Case three years later, destroyed what was left of the spirit of compromise and put the nation firmly on the road to disunion. A new, antislavery political party emerged in response to these events: the Republican Party.

But the growing split between North and South was social and economic as well as political. Southerners were especially disturbed by the growing abolitionist movement in the North, and they were terrified when one of its most radical members, John Brown, led an armed raid in Virginia in 1859.

As the 1850s ended, a movement for secession—separation from the Union—gathered strength in the South. "We cannot stay in the Union," said one Southern senator, "with such dishonor attached to the terms of our remaining." In 1860, the final "dishonor" occurred. In a hotly contested election, Republican Abraham Lincoln won the presidency. A few weeks later, South Carolina became the first Southern state to secede from the Union. America's most bitter conflict—a trial by fire that would last four years and claim hundreds of thousands of lives—was about to begin.

FREE BLACKS

Although many people opposed slavery in pre-Civil War America, few believed that blacks and whites were equal. Free blacks in the North, whether they were born free or had escaped from slavery, generally lived in poverty and had few civil rights. In 1860, for example, only 7 percent of Northern blacks were allowed to vote. Illinois, a free state, even passed a law forbidding free blacks to enter the state.

Many free blacks, however, worked tirelessly for the antislavery cause. Three of the most active black abolitionists were Frederick Douglass, Sojourner Truth, and Harriet Tubman.

The son of a white man and a slave woman, Frederick Douglass was born in Maryland. He escaped to New York in 1838. His career as an abolitionist began three years later, when the Massachusetts Anti-Slavery Society asked him to speak at a meeting. Soon Douglass was denouncing slavery throughout the North in speeches and in his writings.

Like Douglass, Harriet Tubman was born into slavery in Maryland, around 1821. She escaped to the North in 1849. Having tasted freedom herself, she decided to help as many slaves as she could. Tubman made many dangerous trips back into the South, guiding over 300 slaves to freedom along the Underground Railroad.

Sojourner Truth was originally a slave—not in the South, but in New York State. She gained her freedom in 1827 when New York emancipated (freed) its slaves. Sixteen years later she began lecturing against slavery. Her emotional speeches made her one of the most effective abolitionists.

Harriet Tubman (c. 1821–1913; above) made so many missions into the South to free slaves that she earned the nickname "the Moses of her people." At one point, Southern planters offered a $40,000 reward for her capture. During the Civil War, she served as a nurse (and occasional spy) for the Union.

Given the name Isabella Baumfree by her master, Sojourner Truth (c. 1797–1883) chose her own name when she became free. As the title page of her 1850 autobiography (opposite) shows, Sojourner Truth was a former Northern slave. Although Truth's autobiography was factual, abolitionist writers sometimes faked sensational "slave narratives" to win support for their cause.

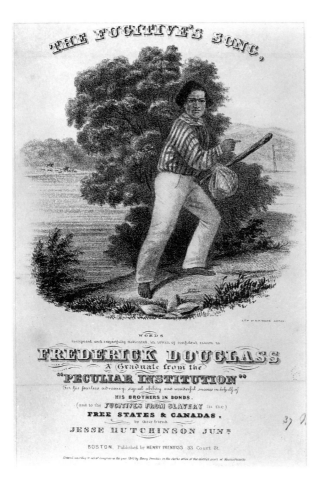

This page of sheet music (left) is for an abolitionist song dedicated to Frederick Douglass (c. 1817–95), "a Graduate from the 'peculiar institution.'" ("Peculiar institution" was a term some Southerners used to describe slavery.) Its composer was Jesse Hutchinson, who was from a family of New England musicians who protested slavery in their songs.

THE UNDERGROUND RAILROAD

Many slaves were willing to risk everything to escape to the free states. Escape involved secretly slipping out of a plantation, then crossing great distances on foot, at night, often with mounted patrols in pursuit. If the runaway reached a free state or territory, he or she might be helped by the Underground Railroad.

The Underground Railroad was a loosely organized network of people including Quakers, abolitionists, and free blacks. To avoid slave catchers, these "conductors" passed escaped slaves from house to house. These houses, called "stations," provided food and clothing, and sometimes forged identity papers for runaways. Most of the stations were in states such as Pennsylvania and Ohio, which bordered the slave states, but the network also reached into New England and upstate New York.

The goal for an escaped slave was to get to a free black community in one of the Northern states. After the passage of the strict Fugitive Slave Act of 1850, however, the Railroad often worked to transport slaves all the way to Canada.

The Underground Railroad, however legendary, was by no means the most important part of a slave's escape. The most dangerous part of the journey to freedom took place before the runaway even reached the Railroad—and that was a journey the fugitive slave usually made all alone.

In this painting (above), escaped slaves reach an Underground Railroad station at Newport, Indiana, in a driving snowstorm. Conductors and fugitives alike scan the area nervously, knowing that slave catchers might not be far behind. The "station-master" here was Levi Coffin, one of the most dedicated white workers on the Railroad.

This frame house (right) was an Underground Railroad station at Canisteo, New York, a town just north of the Pennsylvania border. From here, escaped slaves could travel farther north to Rochester, a community that sheltered many fugitive slaves, or into Canada.

THE KANSAS-NEBRASKA ACT

The next political battle between North and South was sparked not by the issue of slavery but by a railroad route. In 1854, Congress began making plans for a transcontinental railroad to link the West Coast to the eastern part of the nation. For economic reasons, Southern politicians wanted the proposed railroad to run along a southern route. Western politicians wanted a central route through the Great Plains, which would be closer to their home states. One Western politician who favored a central route was Stephen Douglas, a senator from Illinois and the Democratic Party's rising star.

Congress was about to organize a vast stretch of Western land into two territories: Kansas and Nebraska. Since both territories were north of latitude 36' 30", they would be free states, according to the Missouri Compromise. But Douglas proposed letting the citizens of each territory vote on the free/slave question themselves, a process he called "popular sovereignty." He hoped this suggestion would win Southern support for a central railroad route. With backing from Southern congressmen, the revised Kansas-Nebraska Act passed into law.

The Kansas-Nebraska Act met with outrage in the North. It violated the Missouri Compromise, a law that Douglas himself had once called "a sacred thing, which no ruthless hand would ever be reckless enough to disturb." The bitter debate over slavery in the West was on once again.

By the fall of 1855, the antislavery settlers were a majority in Kansas, although proslavery delegates dominated the territorial legislature. In September 1855, a meeting of antislavery Kansans at Big Spring set up a rival government and drafted a state constitution banning slavery. This broadside (above) announces the meeting.

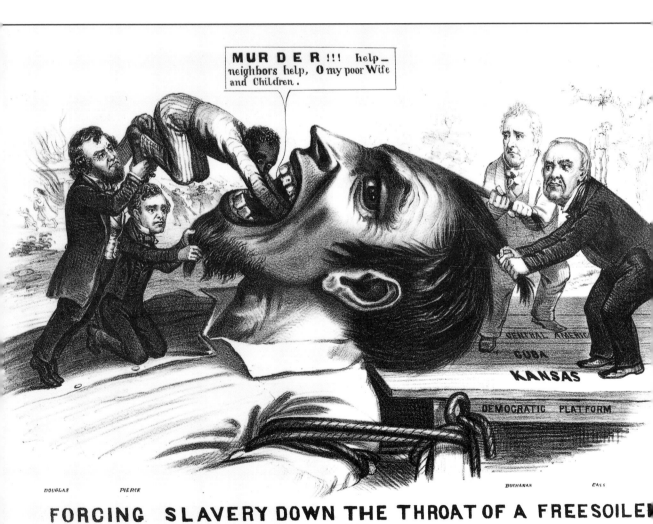

KANSAS: DRESS REHEARSAL FOR CIVIL WAR

After the passage of the Kansas-Nebraska Act, supporters and opponents of slavery rushed into Kansas. (At that time, the vast Nebraska territory attracted few settlers.) Each side hoped to win a majority in the elections for a territorial legislature, and thereby decide the slavery issue. Southern slaveowners who crossed into the territory were dubbed "border ruffians"; antislavery settlers, who came mostly from New England, were nicknamed "free soilers."

Elections for a territorial legislature were held in March 1855. The proslavery faction won a majority, but free soilers charged that the election was a fraud. (It was: Over 6,000 votes were cast, although the territory's voting population was only about 3,000.) But Kansas's federally appointed governor, who favored slavery, upheld the election results. The free soilers refused to accept this ruling. In December 1855, they adopted an antislavery constitution and set up their own government.

Political conflict turned into violence. In May 1856, a proslavery mob destroyed the free-soil town of Lawrence. Four days later, abolitionists led by a fanatic named John Brown killed five proslavery settlers in revenge.

The conflict finally ended in October 1859 when a majority of Kansas settlers ratified a constitution forbidding slavery. On January 29, 1861, Kansas entered the Union as a free state. (Nebraska was not admitted as a state until after the Civil War, in 1867.)

In May 1856, proslavery Kansas judge Samuel Lecompte ordered several abolitionist settlers in Lawrence arrested for "treason." The judge deputized a band of border ruffians to do the job. After dragging five cannons across the prairie, they attacked the town of Lawrence on May 21, as shown in this engraving (opposite, top).

Proslavery "Border Ruffians" menace "Liberty, the Fair Maid of Kansas" in this cartoon protesting popular sovereignty and the chaos it created (opposite, bottom). The "Border Ruffians" shown are in fact prominent Democratic politicians, including President James Buchanan and Illinois senator Stephen Douglas, author of the Kansas-Nebraska Act.

The 800 proslavery attackers not only captured the abolitionists but destroyed Lawrence's hotel and newspaper office, as shown in this newspaper illustration (below). The "sack of Lawrence," as the attack became known, resulted in a bloody reprisal led by the fanatical abolitionist John Brown.

LIBERTY, THE FAIR MAID OF KANSAS—IN THE HANDS OF THE "BORDER RUFFIANS".

THE REPUBLICAN PARTY

The early 1850s were years of frustration for the opponents of slavery. The Kansas-Nebraska Act had largely overturned the "sacred" Missouri Compromise. The nation held together under the Compromise of 1850, but with the provision of the Fugitive Slave Act, there was a desperate need for a new party dedicated to ending slavery, or at least to keeping it from spreading into the West.

In February 1854, a group of antislavery politicians met in a schoolhouse in Ripon, Wisconsin. Some were Northern Democrats. Others were "conscience Whigs," antislavery members of the nation's other major party. Still others belonged to the Free Soil Party. By the end of the meeting, the Republican Party was born.

In the Congressional elections that fall, Republicans managed to win a majority of seats in the House of Representatives. This outcome shocked the Democrats, who were now considered the proslavery party, or at least the party of the South. In the wake of the Republican triumph, many prominent politicians switched parties.

In 1856, the Republicans nominated John C. Frémont, a famous Western explorer and Mexican War hero, for president. The Democratic candidate was James Buchanan of Pennsylvania.

Buchanan won, but the election was close: Frémont trailed Buchanan by only about 500,000 in the popular vote, and he won eleven of the nation's sixteen free states. Buchanan carried the South but won only five free states.

On March 20, 1854, this schoolhouse (opposite, top) in Ripon, Wisconsin, was the site of a protest meeting against the Kansas-Nebraska Act. Historians are uncertain about whether the term "Republican" was first used here, but on May 9 thirty antislavery congressmen formally adopted the name. The first official state Republican Party was founded in Michigan two months later.

This Democratic cartoon (right) shows Republican candidate John C. Frémont (1813–90) mounted on an "abolitionist nag," surrounded by well-known antislavery figures. The party is shown heading for "Salt River"—a nineteenth-century slang term for political defeat.

COⱢ FREMONT'S LAST GRAND EXPLORING EXPEDITION IN 1856.

THE DRED SCOTT CASE

Dred Scott was born a slave in Missouri around 1795. In the 1840s, Scott moved with his master into Illinois and the Minnesota Territory. Illinois was a free state, and slavery was forbidden in Minnesota under the Missouri Compromise. In 1846, Scott sued for his freedom in a Missouri court, claiming that because he lived in a free territory, he was a free man. The court ruled against Scott, as did a federal circuit court. Scott then appealed to the Supreme Court. Southern politicians convinced the Court to hear the case, hoping for a ruling that would protect their legal right to own slaves.

In March 1857, Chief Justice Roger B. Taney announced that Scott, as a slave, was not a citizen and thus had no right to sue in a federal court. According to Taney's majority opinion, blacks "had no rights which the white man was bound to respect." The implications of this decision were broad: If slaves were property, as the court held, then slavery was protected everywhere in the United States, because the Constitution protected private property. Thus, the Missouri Compromise—which most Americans had hoped would settle the question of slavery forever—could now be considered unconstitutional.

The Supreme Court's ruling in *Dred Scott* v. *Sandford* was cheered in the South and denounced in the North. Even newspapers and politicians who were unfriendly to the abolitionists opposed the court's decision. Throughout the United States, people realized that the era of compromises was over.

These engravings (above) show Dred Scott and his wife. When Scott's master, army officer John Emerson, died in 1846, white friends convinced Scott to demand freedom. This suggestion started an eleven-year chain of events leading to the famous Supreme Court decision. Scott himself died in 1858.

Roger Brooke Taney (1777–1864) served as chief justice of the U.S. Supreme Court for twenty-eight years—the longest term of any chief justice. Despite his opposition to what he called "Northern aggression" over slavery, he stayed on the court after the outbreak of war. Taney died in 1864.

ABRAHAM LINCOLN

Abraham Lincoln's grandparents were among the pioneers who moved west over the Appalachian Mountains after the Revolutionary War. They left Virginia for Kentucky, where, on February 12, 1809, Abraham Lincoln was born. Later, Lincoln's family moved to Indiana and finally to Illinois.

Lincoln had little schooling, but he fed his appetite for learning by reading whatever books he could find. At age twenty-three, after trying several business ventures, he ran unsuccessfully for the Illinois legislature. That same year, he served as a militia captain in a minor Indian war, but saw no fighting. He returned to politics in 1834, this time winning a seat as a Whig. Lincoln served in the legislature until 1841, building up a law practice between sessions. (Despite the popular image of Lincoln as a simple frontier lawyer, he made a fortune as an attorney for railroads and other corporations.) In 1842, Lincoln married Mary Todd of Kentucky.

Lincoln first entered national politics in 1846. As a Whig in the House of Representatives, he opposed the war with Mexico. In 1854, Lincoln ran for the Senate, but he was defeated. Two years later, he joined the newly formed Republican Party.

Lincoln was far from being an abolitionist, but his antislavery opinions grew stronger after the passage of the Kansas-Nebraska Act. In 1858, he decided to challenge the author of the bill, fellow Illinois lawyer Stephen Douglas, for his seat in the Senate.

This early portrait shows a clean-shaven Abraham Lincoln. He grew his famous beard in 1860, at the suggestion of an eleven-year-old girl who saw him at a campaign appearance. Lincoln liked to joke about his rough-hewn looks, once saying that "God must love plain-looking people—he made so many of them."

THE LINCOLN-DOUGLAS DEBATES

The Illinois senate race of 1858 drew national attention. As Abraham Lincoln and Stephen Douglas campaigned, people everywhere realized that the major issue of the election—slavery in the territories—could determine the future of the entire nation.

Lincoln accepted the Republican senatorial nomination and opened his campaign with a powerful speech on June 16, 1858. "A house divided against itself cannot stand," he declared, paraphrasing the Bible. "I believe this government cannot endure permanently half slave and half free . . . it will become all one thing or all the other." Douglas rose to Lincoln's challenge. The two lawyer-politicians—who, years before, had argued opposite sides in a murder case—agreed to face off in a series of debates from August to October.

Douglas vigorously defended his belief in popular sovereignty. The people of each territory, Douglas repeated, should decide for themselves whether or not to allow slavery. Douglas also accused Lincoln of placing too much emphasis on the slavery issue and the rights of blacks. Lincoln, however, argued that slavery was a moral issue, while Douglas continued to treat it as a matter of practical politics.

When the votes were counted, Lincoln lost the election by a small margin. Douglas kept his Senate seat. Despite his defeat, Lincoln emerged from the debates as the nation's leading antislavery politician.

Stephen Douglas (1813–61; above), known as "the little giant" for his small stature but powerful political influence, was a champion of Western expansion and a supporter of the Mexican War prior to his senatorial career. Despite the fact that he was defeated by Lincoln in the 1860 presidential race, he was an ardent supporter of the Lincoln administration until his death in 1861.

This drawing (right) depicts the August 27 debate between Lincoln and Douglas at Freeport, Illinois. Fifteen thousand people attended. It was here that Douglas, under pressure from Lincoln, proclaimed the "Freeport Doctrine"—based on his opinion that territories should make their own laws concerning slavery, regardless of the Dred Scott decision.

JOHN BROWN

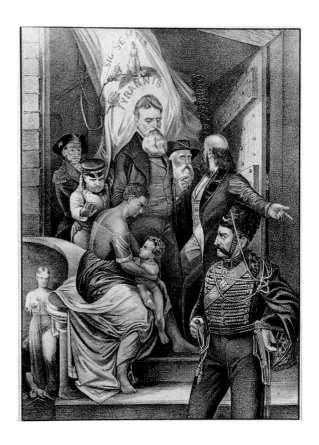

John Brown was born in Torrington, Connecticut, in 1800. He tried several business careers without success. But Brown was also a fanatically religious man who believed that God had given him a mission in life: to free the slaves. It was in Kansas that Brown's capacity for brutal violence surfaced. In May 1856, Brown and four of his sons led a massacre in Potawatomie, in which five proslavery settlers were murdered in cold blood.

In 1858, Brown traveled to New England seeking money for a new project. He planned to carve out a stronghold in the Appalachian Mountains. From there he planned to lead raids to free slaves throughout the South. Most abolitionists recognized Brown for the fanatic he was, but several agreed to finance his scheme.

On the night of October 16, 1859, Brown and seventeen followers captured the federal arsenal at Harpers Ferry, Virginia, in order to seize weapons. The next morning, Colonel Robert E. Lee of the U.S. Army assembled a force of Marines and left Washington for Harpers Ferry. By nightfall of the following day, the arsenal was back in federal hands. Ten of Brown's followers died in the fight. Brown himself was wounded and captured.

Brown was tried for treason by a Virginia court, found guilty, and hanged on December 2, 1859. Brown's calm defense of his actions during the trial—and the brave manner in which he faced his death—impressed many people in the North. Within months, many prominent abolitionists were hailing Brown as a martyr in the fight against slavery.

In this fanciful lithograph (above), a slave woman asks John Brown (1800–59) to bless her child as the radical abolitionist walks calmly to his execution. (The incident did not actually take place.) After Brown's "martyrdom," Ralph Waldo Emerson described him as "that new saint . . . who will make the gallows glorious like the cross."

Marines used ladders to break down the doors of the firehouse where Brown and his band had barricaded themselves at Harpers Ferry, as shown in this wood-engraving (right). Brown and his "officers" killed four people, including a free black railroad worker whose train stopped at the town's station while the raid was in progress.

THE ELECTION OF 1860

The presidential election of 1860 brought the tensions over slavery to a head. Many Southerners in Congress said that if an "unacceptable" candidate were elected, they would urge their states to secede from the Union.

In May, the Republicans met in Chicago. The abolitionist wing of the party favored Senator William Seward of New York, but Abraham Lincoln finally won the nomination. Although Lincoln was in Illinois during the convention, his political allies won the nomination for him without his knowledge, mainly by offering cabinet posts and other rewards to powerful politicians who promised their support.

The Democratic Party fell apart at its Baltimore convention. Most of the party's Southern delegates walked out after the party leadership tried to downplay the slavery issue. These breakaway delegates nominated Vice President John C. Breckinridge, a Kentuckian, as their candidate. The remaining Democrats selected Stephen Douglas, Lincoln's former opponent.

When the votes were counted on November 6, Lincoln had won only 1,866,452 popular votes. Together, his two rivals received 2,815,617. But the split in the Democratic Party gave Lincoln 180 electoral votes; the closest runner-up in the electoral college, Breckinridge, received only 72. Thus, Lincoln was a "minority president"—although he was the winner, he began his administration knowing that the majority of American voters had supported other candidates.

John Cabell Breckinridge (1821–75; above) was the presidential candidate nominated by the Southern Democrats. Defeated in the presidential election, he returned to Washington, D.C., as a senator from Kentucky. After his pro-Confederate position led to a warrant for his arrest in 1861, Breckinridge fled the capital and became a general in the Confederate Army.

This cartoon (right), titled "Uncle Sam Making New Arrangements," was probably printed in the last days of the 1860 campaign, when a Republican victory seemed likely. It shows Uncle Sam turning away Bell, Breckinridge, and Douglas from the door of the White House, saying, "You're too late gentlemen, I've concluded . . . to let Abraham Lincoln have the place."

The Republicans made Abraham Lincoln's humble background a major part of their campaign. This illustration (left) shows him splitting fence rails. (Lincoln had worked as a rail-splitter as a young man.)

THE FIRST STATES SECEDE

South Carolina had been on the front line of the South's political battles with the North since the Nullification Crisis of 1833. Now that Abraham Lincoln was president of the United States, South Carolina led the South in its break from the Union.

On December 20, 1860, the state's leading citizens gathered in Charleston. They voted unanimously "that the union now subsisting between South Carolina and other states under the name of the United States of America is hereby dissolved."

South Carolina's bold action met with mixed responses in the South. Many Southerners applauded and called for their own states to do the same—if only to frighten the federal government into changing the laws to protect slavery. Others hesitated at the idea of a permanent break with the Union. The secessionists were actually a minority in much of the South, but they were better organized and more vocal than the "cooperationists" who favored staying in the Union.

On January 9, 1861, Mississippi became the second state to secede. By the end of January, four more states—Florida, Alabama, Georgia, and Louisiana—had left the Union. Texas, the first Western state to secede, did so on March 2, the day before Lincoln's inauguration. Texas's break came despite the efforts of Senator Sam Houston, who fought to keep the state in the Union that it had struggled so long to join.

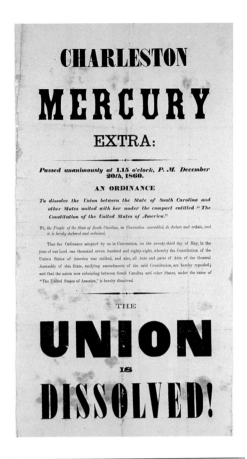

The Charleston Mercury, *Charleston's leading newspaper, always supported the cause of "Southern rights." On December 20, 1860, the* Mercury *celebrated South Carolina's secession with a full-page headline anouncing, "The Union is Dissolved!"*

This pro-Union cartoon (opposite, top), titled "The Secession Movement," depicts the leaders of five seceding Southern states (South Carolina, Florida, Alabama, Mississippi, and Louisiana) riding on pigs and jackasses toward a cliff. Their leader, South Carolina, reaches for a butterfly labeled "Secessionist Humbug." The sixth figure, who rides along a slightly different path, represents Georgia.

In this wood-engraving (right), Charleston residents greet the news of the state's secession with cheers. "There is nothing in all the dark caves of human passion so cruel and deadly," a British reporter wrote at the time, "as the hatred the South Carolinians profess for the Yankees."

JEFFERSON DAVIS

The man who would one day govern the Confederacy was born in rural Kentucky in 1808. His family moved to Mississippi, where they established a small but prosperous cotton plantation. After graduating from West Point in 1828, Davis served seven years on the frontier before resigning from the army to marry Sarah Taylor, daughter of future president Zachary Taylor. Sarah died three months after the wedding. Grief stricken, Davis bought a Mississippi plantation and spent the next decade raising cotton and studying law. He married his second wife, Varina Howell, in 1845.

Davis returned to the army with the outbreak of the Mexican War. As commander of a regiment of Mississippi volunteers, he won a reputation as a brave and effective leader. After the war, Davis (a Democrat) represented Mississippi in the Senate.

In 1853, President Franklin Pierce appointed Davis secretary of war. In 1858, after Pierce left office, Davis returned to Washington as a senator. In his early political career, Davis was more moderate than many Southern leaders. Following Lincoln's election, however, he resigned his post. Davis always considered himself a soldier first, and he hoped to be named commander of the Confederate Army. But on February 10, 1861, a messenger appeared at Brierfield, Davis's plantation. The letter he carried began: "Sir: We . . . inform you that you are this day unanimously elected President of the Provisional Government of the Confederate States of America."

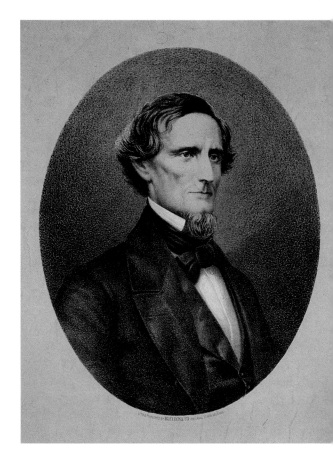

As a former soldier, Jefferson Davis (above) knew the South would have to fight for its independence. "The time for compromise has passed," he said shortly after arriving at the Confederate Convention at Montgomery, Alabama. "The South is determined to maintain her position, and make all who oppose her smell Southern powder and feel Southern steel."

On February 18, 1861, Jefferson Davis took the oath of office as the first (and only) president of the Confederate States of America. The ceremony took place at the temporary Confederate capital at Montgomery, Alabama, as shown in this engraving. Later in the year, the Confederate government moved to Richmond, Virginia.

THE BIRTH OF THE CONFEDERACY

On February 4, 1861, delegates from the six states that had seceded met in Montgomery, Alabama, to form the government of a new nation—the Confederate States of America.

Within a week, the delegates drafted and adopted a constitution. The document was similar to the Constitution of the United States, but it specifically protected slavery and the "sovereign and independent capacity" of each state. The Confederate Constitution also gave the president a six-year term. On February 9, the Confederate Convention named Jefferson Davis president and elected Alexander Stephens (1812–83) of Georgia vice president. Finally, the convention scheduled elections throughout the Confederacy to elect Davis and Stephens formally and to choose members for the new nation's senate and house of representatives.

Davis arrived in Montgomery on the night of February 17. A cheering crowd greeted him, along with a band playing "Dixie"—a song that soon became the Confederacy's unofficial anthem. As Davis rose to give his first speech as president of the new nation, William L. Yancey of Alabama, one of the South's fiercest secessionists, shouted, "The man and the hour have met!"

Davis immediately set to work. His task was formidable. Aside from overseeing the organization of a new national government, Davis had to prepare to meet whatever challenge the Union chose to make.

As this map shows (opposite, top), the eleven states that eventually made up the Confederate States of America did not all leave the Union at the same time. Six states (shown in green) seceded before the attack on Fort Sumter in April 1861; the states of the upper South (shown in orange) waited until after the war started before deciding to secede. The map also shows which Union states still permitted slavery (shown in purple) and which were free (shown in pink). The regions in yellow indicate territory controlled by the federal government but not yet made into states.

The title of this cartoon (right) is "The Dis-United States, or the Southern Confederacy." It portrays the Southern leaders as a group of selfish politicians hoping to advance their states' interests at the expense of the nation. The cartoon was published at about the same time that the Confederate Convention met at Montgomery.

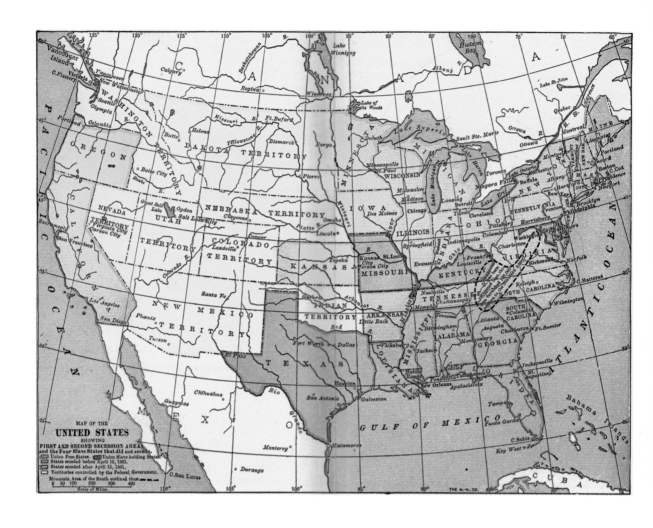

Map of the
UNITED STATES
SHOWING
FIRST AND SECOND SECESSION AREAS
and the Four Slave States that did not secede.

LINCOLN TAKES OFFICE

On February 11, 1861, Abraham Lincoln left Springfield, Illinois, and boarded a train for Washington. It was the last time he would see his home.

The journey took almost two weeks. Lincoln made many speeches along the way, but he said little about what was most on people's minds: his plans for dealing with the secession crisis. He was so vague that Northern newspapers nicknamed him "President Facing-both-ways."

Lincoln arrived in Philadelphia on February 22. There he heard that Allan Pinkerton, the nation's most famous detective, had uncovered an assassination plot. The president-elect reluctantly agreed to travel the final and most dangerous leg of the trip—through largely pro-Confederate Maryland—in secret. Lincoln finally arrived in Washington early on the morning of February 23.

On the cold, windy morning of March 4, 1861, Abraham Lincoln strode up the Capitol steps to take the oath of office. In his inaugural address, he stated that he had no wish to abolish slavery where it already existed, but that he believed that secession was unconstitutional. "A husband and wife may be divorced, and go . . . beyond the reach of each other; but the different parts of our country cannot do this." Stating that war would come only if the South fired the first shot, Lincoln made his stand clear. "You have no oath registered in heaven to destroy the government, while I shall have the most solemn one to 'preserve, protect, and defend' it."

This photograph shows Lincoln's inauguration on March 4, 1861. Government officials feared an assassination attempt at the ceremony. Army sharpshooters were posted on nearby rooftops, their rifles trained on the crowd of 10,000 people, while cavalry patrolled Pennsylvania Avenue.

THE FORT SUMTER CRISIS

The most pressing crisis facing Lincoln was one he inherited from James Buchanan, the previous president. The crisis concerned Fort Sumter, a federal post at Charleston, South Carolina.

On December 20, 1860, as South Carolina's state convention voted for secession, U.S. Army major Robert Anderson and seventy-three soldiers occupied the fort. State authorities took possession of the other forts around Charleston and ordered Anderson and his men to leave. Buchanan ordered them to stay. He did so over the protests of many politicians, including the pro-South secretary of war, John Floyd, who soon resigned.

Cut off from shore, the fort could hold out only as long as its supplies lasted. On January 9, the *Star of the West*, a merchant ship hired to bring supplies and reinforcements to Fort Sumter, reached Charleston Harbor. Artillery manned by South Carolina state militia opened fire, and the *Star of the West* headed back north.

After taking office, Lincoln quickly decided that Fort Sumter would not be abandoned. Although his own secretary of state, William Seward, stated that the garrison would be withdrawn, Lincoln ordered another relief expedition in early April. Before it could arrive, the Confederate government sent a message to Major Anderson: Surrender the fort or face an attack. Anderson refused to give in.

On the night of April 11, Confederate shore batteries took careful aim and waited for the signal to open fire. At 4:30 a.m. on April 12, it came.

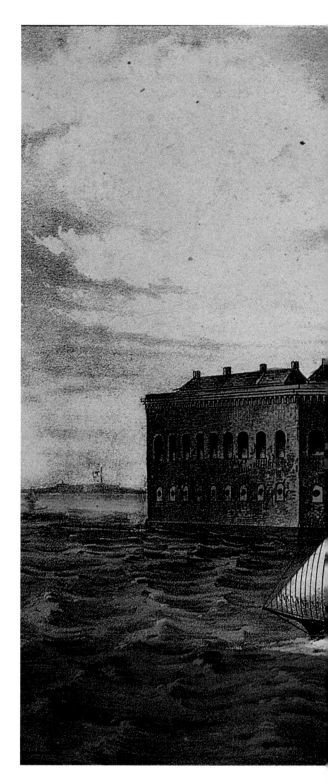

Fort Sumter, whose brick walls rose forty feet above a man-made island in Charleston Harbor, was completed only a short time before South Carolina's secession. Although the fort was built to house 650 soldiers and 150 cannons, fewer than one hundred soldiers manned it when the siege began. This lithograph depicts the fort in peacetime.

Resource Guide

Key to picture positions: (T) top, (C) center, (B) bottom; and in combinations: (TL) top left, (TR) top right, (BL) bottom left, (BR) bottom right, (RC) right center, (LC) left center.

Key to picture locations within the Library of Congress collections (and where available, photo negative numbers): P - Prints and Photographs Division; R - Rare Book Division; G - General Collections; MSS - Manuscript Division; G&M - Geography and Map Division

PICTURES IN THIS VOLUME

2–3 Plantation, P **4–5** soap label, P **6–7** farm, P **8–9** map, G

Timeline: **10–11** TL, boat, G; BL, Monroe, G; TR, canal, P; BR, title page, G **12–13** TL, Santa Anna, G; LC, Black Hawk, P; BL, Turner, P, USZ62-2580; TR, battle, G **14–15** TL, slaves, P; BL, Tyler, P, USZ62-290; BR, map, G **16–17** TL, Brady, P; BL, Uncle Tom, P, USZ62-30877; TR, Garibaldi, G

Part I: **18–19** presidents, P USZ62-83788 **20–21** TL, Monroe, G; TR, Washington, P, USA7-35644; BR, Adams, P **22–23** TL, tobacco, P, USZ62-72333; TR, cotton, P, USZ62-69178 **24–25** TL, Jefferson, G; TR, title page, G **26–27** TL, Clay, P; CL, Webster, P; TR, map, G; BL, Randolph, G **28–29** TR, Beacon Hill, P, USZC4-682; BC, Merchant Exchange, P **30–31** TL, factory workers, P; BL, arms plant, P, USZC4-773; TR, title page, P **32–33** TR, riverboat, P; BC, dock, P **34–35** BL, field, P, USZ62-12848; TR, Whitney, P, USZ62-8282 **36–37** TL, Calhoun, G; BR, cartoon, G **38–39** TR, meeting, G; BC, pioneer home, P **40–41** TR, Polk, P; BC, Battle of Mexico, P **42–43** TL, Chapultepec, P; TR, campaign poster, P, USZ62-91513; BR, dragoons, P **44–45** TL, flag, R; TR, gold, P; BR, San Francisco, R **46–47** Senate, P **48–49** TL, broadside, MSS; TR, Burns, P, USZ62-90750; BR, cartoon, P, USZ62-89722 **50–51** TL, massacre, P, USZ62-33457; BC, cartoon, USZ62-1285 **52–53** slave, P, USZ62-

90345; BR, kidnapping, P, USZ62-30832 **54–55** TL, Garrison, P, BH2201-5004A; TR, title page, R; BR, newspaper masthead, P **56–57** TL, declaration, P, USZ62-40758; BR, meeting, P, USZ62-37574 **58–59** TL, title page, P, USZ62-60868; TR, Know-Nothings, P, USZ62-31070; BR, strike, P, USZ62-8384 **60–61** TL, Stowe, P, USZ62-10476; TR, celebration, P, USZ62-33468; TR, playbill, P, USZC4-1298

Part II: **62–63** campaign flag, P, USZC2-331 **64–65** TL, Tubman, P; TR, Douglass, P, USZ62-7823; BR, Truth, R **66–67** TR, escape, P, USZ62-28860; BR, house, USZ62-15257 **68–69** TL, broadside, G; BR, cartoon, P, USZ62-29043 **70–71** BL, ruins, P, USZ62-53868; TR, massacre, P, USZ62-33382; BR, cartoon, P, USZ62-92023 **72–73** TR, house, P; BR, cartoon, P, USZ62-7785 **74–75** TR, Taney, P, USZ62-25516; BR, Scott and wife, R **76–77** TR, Lincoln, P, USZ62-7728A **78–79** TL, Douglas, P; TR, debate, P, USZ62-29291 **80–81** TL, Brown, P; BR, engine house, P, USZ62-2893 **82–83** TL, Breckinridge, P; TR, Lincoln, P; BR, cartoon, P, USZ62-12424 **84–85** TL, newspaper, P; TR, cartoon, P, USZ62-32995; BR, Charleston, P, USZ62-14946 **86–87** TL, Davis, P; BR, inauguration, P, USZC4-1498 **88–89** TR, map, G; BR, cartoon, P, USZ62-92048 **90–91** inauguration, P, USZ62-15117 **92–93** Ft. Sumter, P

SUGGESTED READING

BATTY, PETER AND PETER PARISH. *The Divided Union.* Topsfield, MA: Salem House, 1987.

CATTON, BRUCE. *The American Heritage Picture History of the Civil War.* New York: Bonanza Books, 1982.

FOMER, ERIC AND OLIVIA MAHONEY. *A House Divided.* Chicago: Chicago Historical Society, 1990.

SMITH, CARTER. *The Civil War.* New York: Facts on File, 1989.

TIME-LIFE. *Brother Against Brother.* New York: Prentice Hall, 1990.

Index

Page numbers in *italics* indicate illustrations